English Bottles and Decanters 1650–1900

Derek C. Davis

English Bottles and Decanters
1650-1900

The World Publishing Company
New York

Published by The World Publishing Company

Published simultaneously in Canada
by Nelson, Foster & Scott Ltd.

First American Edition 1972

WORLD PUBLISHING
TIMES MIRROR

Contents

English Bottles and Decanters 1650-1900

INTRODUCTION

There is something in the nature of glass which has held the fascination of many people over many thousands of years. The stages in the development of what we know to be glass, though widely interspaced by many centuries, are not very many. On the other hand, the history of the use of glass and of the achievements of glassmakers is tortuous, and its study is full of pitfalls. Too often we are inclined to accept notions and vague fancies of would-be historians whilst we are confronted equally often with a lack of facts. Romance is sometimes more palatable than cold chronology, and somehow even when one has learned the facts a little romance still seems to creep in, particularly if one is a collector. This short introduction to the history of glassmaking is intended mainly to give some perspective to the period and subject of our interest, namely bottles and decanters from circa 1650 to the late 19th century.

The first use of an artificially produced glassy substance can be dated as early as 4000 B.C. From this time, in Egypt and Mesopotamia, stones and ceramics were being coated with glaze, and while the formula of glaze differs from that of glass, it is still a glass recipe. As an independent substance, glass seems to date from somewhere in the third millennium B.C. and to have been manufactured first in Mesopotamia, although glass vessels do not appear much before 1500 B.C. King Tuthmosis III of Egypt invaded and began conquering Assyria in 1481 B.C., and as part of his booty is presumed to have brought back to Egypt both glasses and glass workers from the industry in Assyria. Judging by the products which soon appeared, the new medium was much to the taste of the Egyptians who applied to it their established skill with furnaces and in chemistry. The result was a series of vases in shapes mostly derived from pottery and faïence and in a wide range of glowing colours with complex decorations in mixtures of contrasting shades. Luckily for us the workers may have wanted to honour the Pharaoh by including his name on the vessels, three of which survive giving glass historians their first definite dating of between 1504 and 1450 B.C., the period of this King's reign. The glasses were made by building a 'core' of varying mixtures of mud and probably straw, to the required shape, at the end of a metal rod. This was then dipped in molten glass and smoothed on a stone slab or 'marver', the process being repeated until the glass was sufficiently thick and smooth. Coloured threads or blobs of glass were applied to the surface of the vessel, heated and marvered in, having been tooled or combed for differing effects. Feet and handles were added before the rod and core were removed. The industry flourished in Egypt and Mesopotamia for about three hundred years until about 1200 B.C. when tremendous political upheavals and natural disasters interrupted culture all over the Eastern Mediterranean, bringing, naturally, a distinct lull in glass vessel production, and in Egypt an almost total cessation for many centuries. A small number of glasses continued to be made in this technique throughout the Mediterranean, but it was not until around the 9th to 8th centuries B.C. that a revival in glass production began in Syria and Mesopotamia. New political influences and artistic tastes stimulated craftsmen, and Phoenician traders were active in spreading both the goods and the ideas. By the 6th century B.C. core-formed glasses were being made all over the Eastern Mediterranean with Graeco/Persian taste in shape and colour predominating. Other techniques had also been developed, such as casting in closed or open moulds, and grinding and cutting from raw blocks. Alexandria, the great centre of learning, culture, and industry had been founded by Alexander the Great in 332 B.C. The enormous reputation of the city, and the flow of ideas and skills brought about by widespread trade and Hellenistic conquests, attracted the best artisans, and some of the finest glasswares in many varied techniques, which date from the third century B.C. are presumed to have come from here.

Glass Blowing

The earliest blown glasses known form a small group of simple bottles dating from about 150 B.C. which were found in an Etruscan tomb. However it was not until about 50 B.C. that the most important advances took place in the technique of inflating glass through a hollow metal pipe, and we must look farther East to Syria and especially Sidon for the finest early developments. The simplicity of the technique is astonishing, and it has hardly changed over the centuries, with tools similar to those of the earliest craftsmen still being used today. The Sidonian craftsmen seem quickly to have become specialists in inflating glass, and by about 50 A.D. were producing fine elaborate vessels blown into moulds. The glasses emerged not only with beautiful relief decorations but sometimes with the names of the early workers and the name of Sidon included in the design. Glass blowing spread rapidly throughout the Roman Empire with the tradition of restraint coupled with luxury inherited from Alexandria resulting in such treasures as the Portland Vase in the British Museum and the Ennion Vase in the Corning Glass Center. By the second and third centuries A.D. thousands of glasses were being made all over the ancient world with regional centres growing up and beginning to produce specialities. Cologne in Germany became an important producer of exciting and sumptuous glasses. Vessels decorated with wandering 'snake threads', others scratched with figurative scenes, and impressive carved, layered, and faceted glasses must have brought the city deserved fame. It is interesting for us to note how early began the practice of cutting and faceting, so important in the decoration of drinking glasses and decanters of our main period of interest. Carving from solid blocks or thick blanks had been practised in Egypt and by Achaemenian artisans with obvious success many centuries earlier, but finds from Cologne have brought to light glass bowls and bottles

8

with fine faceted decoration in numbers hitherto unknown. The usual pattern of Eastern innovations spreading to greater successes in the West seems reversed in this case, for the technique died out in Germany, but a succession of superb carved and faceted glasses has survived from the third and fourth centuries onwards in the East. The Sassanians carried the technique farther eastwards, producing deeply cut, beautifully coloured bowls and chalices. The genius of Islamic craftsmen from eighth century Baghdad, and Egypt and Persia of the tenth century, poured their energies into a host of decorative glassmaking techniques, notably moulding, faceting and cutting, and later enamelling and gilding.

Islamic Glass

Glassmaking was a flourishing and complex industry in the lands conquered by the followers of Islam during the seventh and eighth centuries A.D. Styles did not immediately change from the elaboration and richness of Byzantine glasses, nor the subtlety of the Parthian and Sassanian workshops, but gradually a fusion took place under the dictates of the creed and the demands of the patrons. From the eighth century, glasses which one can call distinctly Islamic begin to emerge from Baghdad and Egypt. So famous were the cut glasses and crystals of Egypt and Mesopotamia that examples are found in municipal and ecclesiastical treasuries in many parts of Europe. Techniques inherited from the Ancient, Byzantine, and Sassanian worlds were transformed and developed, in particular lustre painting, gilding, and enamelling. Gilding and enamelling of glass was a practice which was to have an enormous influence in Europe. Basically, the decoration of opaque vitreous enamels was applied to already formed glasses which were then fired for fixing. The principal centres of production were in the Near East, and the most renowned glasses which spread as far as China and England were made in Syria during the thirteenth and fourteenth centuries. Through trade, the conquests of the Crusades which began in the eleventh century, and the great Venetian Empire which grew up, Europe began to see many different objects from the East, in particular fabrics, pottery, Saracenic metalware, and the glasses of Syria. Venice quite possibly imported Byzantine glass blowers for her own infant industry, but at first the port was more important as the European clearing house for Middle Eastern products. A dramatic turn in Syrian history proved the greatest awakener to the Eastern influenced Venetian glass industry, for in 1402 Tamerlane attacked Damascus, and captured and destroyed this great centre of learning and industry. The glass craftsmen were banished and the industry virtually extinguished, thus cutting Europe off from a major source of glass. It is possible that Venice managed to protect and import some of these workers, for within twenty or thirty years her home industry was established, and she had virtual control of the European glass market.

Early Western European Developments

It must not be forgotten, however, that significant if less dramatic developments were taking place in Western Europe from the fourth century onwards. During the

Roman occupation, glass-producing centres in France and Germany had flourished, and after the empire crumbled these centres continued to make wares, but in much changed form to suit Teutonic tastes. Few Roman decorative techniques survived, save moulding and trailing, the latter being used to quite elaborate and exquisite effect. In about the tenth century the glassmakers began to use sources of alkali in their glass batches or mixtures, derived from bracken and other woodland plants, and the typical dark-age wares have come to be called 'forest-glass' or Waldglas, or 'bracken-glass' or *Verre de fougère*. The glass is mostly greenish or dark brown with a limited form range of cups, drinking-horns, and cone beakers, of which the last are perhaps the most famous being sometimes massively ornamented with claw-like prunts. Although traces of Roman glassworks have been found in England, as widely dispersed as Wilderspool near Warrington, Colchester, and London, no centres have as yet been identified with certainty as dating from the period immediately after the Roman withdrawal, and glass has not been found in great quantities in Anglo-Saxon cemeteries. The early industry in England does not seem to have been either widespread or very active, for Bede, who lived between 673 and 735, records that glassworkers had to be imported to England from Gaul to make windows for churches and also to teach the English the craft. King Stephen (1135–1154) made Henry Daniel vitrearius, Prior at the Monastery of Holme in Norfolk, and there were also various requests to the Continent for glass workers, and so we may presume that the English soon forgot or did not care for the occupation. In English glass history of this time the most important indication of events and of the future is the arrival from Normandy in 1226 of a craftsman named Laurence Vitrearius, who settled at Dyers Cross, near Chiddingfold, by the well-wooded Surrey-Sussex border. Here he began manufacturing *Verre de fougère* similar to the Waldglas of Germany. Laurence 'the glassworker' seems primarily to have been a window-glass maker, and it is recorded that by about 1240 he was making glass for Westminster Abbey. Laurence and his son, now called William le Verrir, must have been successful, for they founded a glass-manufacturing industry in this area which lasted until the early-seventeenth century. Their immediate successors, John de Alemayen and Richard Holmere, continued making the greenish white window-glass for ecclesiastical buildings, but also made 'urynalls, bottles, bowles, cuppis to drink, and such lyke' for the local market. The practice of making simple vessels alongside window-glass seems to be usual, and although it was presumed that there was a wide range of items, very few have survived.

There had existed in Venice as early as 1224 a glass-blowers' guild, and it was known that they could make 'graceful objects'. Presumably some of the skills had been learnt in Constantinople from Byzantine glass workers. Eastern trade had interested not only the Venetians. Genoa and Catalonia were competitors in the field, the latter being also notable for producing simple serviceable glass. The prevailing styles in glasses in these areas are not distinctive, and have been referred to by Barrington-Haynes as '*façon-de-Syrie*', sometimes 'confused with Mohammedan glass'. It is generally thought that an independent Venetian style in glass begins after 1450. At first the finest glasses were richly coloured pedestal-footed goblets in Gothic style heightened with gilding and gem-like enamel dots. The glass trade prospered and very soon the Venetians had developed a bewildering array of glasses in a wide range of complicated decorative techniques. The secrets of the glass-houses were heavily guarded, and severe penalties threatened workmen who attempted to leave and work elsewhere, but foreign rulers wanted glassmaking industries of their own, and doubtless the Venetians were willing to risk being seduced by enormous bribes, for glasses almost indistinguishable from the Venetian wares began to be made in Germany, Bohemia, the Netherlands, and England by the sixteenth century, the wares being called *façon de Venise*. France did not seem to have much success at that time in glass making despite her early traditions dating from the Roman era and the medieval exports of window-glass from Normandy. Spain also had a tradition going back to Roman times, and fared better. The Catalonians, as mentioned before, had a share in Eastern trade, and were making good glass in the fifteenth to sixteenth centuries. In the seventeenth and eighteenth centuries the Moorish-influenced styles of Andalucia and Granada appeared in surprisingly original and indeed rather fantastic forms. The Netherlands had also been brought up on a tradition of glasses going back to the Roman occupation of the Rhinelands, and one of the most distinctive types of glasses which originated here and which enjoyed a very long lasting success, were the 'roemers'—derived from the Waldglas beakers which through the centuries developed, changed and modified with a metal improvement which kept apace with the designs. In this part of Europe Venetian style glass was first made at Antwerp in the middle of the sixteenth century, followed by Liège, Rotterdam, and Amsterdam. The Spanish occupation and persecutions were not conducive to an active trade in luxury goods, and later competition from Germany and England did not aid the industry. Nevertheless some of the finest quality and most beautifully engraved glasses originated from the Netherlands from the mid-sixteenth century on. Certainly the Dutch glass-makers so accurately copied the glasses of Venice that they are often difficult to tell apart. The Venetian craftsmen first found their way into Germany, arriving in the Tyrol, but though they were welcomed, the taste, as in Bohemia, was for more sturdy glasses out of the Waldglas tradition. Wonderful enamelled glasses were a speciality made in the fifteenth and sixteenth centuries, particularly in Nuremburg, and clear and gilt glasses came from Potsdam, and, subsequent to the introduction of engraving, some of the finest glasses decorated in this manner were made in Germany. The pattern of later glassmaking throughout Europe was much the same; the beginnings were characterized by a primitive medieval manufacture progressing through trials and failures until the establishment of a glass similar to that of Venice, and from there the emergence of something more of a native style. The great expansion and output of Venice during the sixteenth century began to decline with the century. With increasing outside competition, the loss of workers, and the trading and territorial losses of the state, the industry began to fade.

John Carré and the Lorrainers

Some of the most active competition for the Venetians was coming from the Lorrainers and Huguenots of Normandy. These workers were being attracted to

England, partly, in the case of the former group, because of over-production in Lorraine, and also because in England there was a degree of peace and their Protestant faith would not incur penalties. Notwithstanding these rather oversimplified reasons it was, as we have seen with Laurence Vitrearius, nothing new for glassmakers to come from Europe to England. 'The astute Antwerp promoter', John Carré was largely responsible for the introduction of large numbers of Lorrainers into England. In 1567 Carré petitioned Queen Elizabeth for a monopolistic licence to make vessel glass in the Venetian style in London. He did not obtain this, but was permitted to make 'glas for glasinge' on condition that he paid a royalty and trained Englishmen in the craft. Wood shortage encouraged other Lorrainers and Normans to move farther West and North where they began to devise means of using coal. Carré set up a factory in the Surrey–Sussex area, but more importantly succeeded in setting up in London a crystal-glass factory, run by Lorrainers, to manufacture Venetian glass. Into this Crutched Friars factory, Carré introduced Venetian glassmakers, one of whom was Jacopo Verzelini (1522–1606) who eventually succeeded in obtaining the monopoly that Carré had been seeking. In 1575 Queen Elizabeth granted Verzelini a twenty-one-year permission for the manufacture of Venice glass in England. The licence was monopolistic, and to safeguard his position the importation of Venetian glass was forbidden and a fine placed on any glassmaker who infringed his monopoly. The only glasses remaining which are definitely attributable to him are a series of admirable goblets, the earliest (now in the Corning Glass Museum) bearing the date 1577. Verzelini retired in 1592 and the remainder of his contract was taken over by a soldier and company promoter Sir Jerome Bowes.

The problem of wood shortage had become somewhat acute by the beginning of the seventeenth century, not only for glassmakers and metal workers, but also for the navy. In 1615 Sir Robert Mansell, who as a retired admiral had a special interest in the preservation of remaining woods for ship building, joined forces with Thomas Percival whose experiments with using coal in the glass furnaces were supposed to have met with some success. The process must have worked, for in 1623 the pair had obtained the sole right to make 'all manner of drinking glasses . . . all other kinds of glasses, bugles, bottles, vials, or vessels whatsoever'. The royal proclamation forbidding the use of wood in glassmaking had a considerable effect on the wandering manufacturers of common domestic glass. The luxury trade prospered, however, and Venice glasses were of such quality as to cause the Venetian Ambassador to write home in admiration of the accomplishments of the English workers. At the death of Mansell his monopoly was taken over by the Duke of Buckingham who at the same time maintained his own factory at Greenwich, exercised the sole privilege for making 'mirror plate' in a factory at Vauxhall, and controlled the patents granted to three other crystal-glass makers. The English-made Venice glasses were simpler and less ornamented than their prototypes. It was also noted in 1672, by John Greene, a glass seller, that the English glasses were more easily broken than the true Venetian products. The simplicity of styles in vogue in England are to be seen in designs which the same John Greene sent to Venice when ordering glasses from a Venetian—Morelli—as the Civil War had interrupted much of the English manufacture. The wandering glassmakers, despite the effects of the 1615 wood proclamation continued making coarse glass, including serving bottles, a kind of bottle-decanter, the first known example being made in 1623, but more of that later.

George Ravenscroft and the Glass-of-Lead

The Company of Glaziers had a history going back to 1328, but in 1637 we hear of the Glass Sellers Company in a complaint against the badness of Sir Robert Mansell's glass. This Company received a charter in 1635, and was active in protecting monopolies, and promoting trade especially in relation to the Duke of Buckingham 'who had a finger in every pie containing glass'. Beginning with John Greene, the brittleness of English glass was causing concern, and experiments to change this were being undertaken. An analytical chemist, George Ravenscroft, as a result of continuous experimenting began one of the most important changes in glassmaking. Ravenscroft introduced an oxide of lead as part of the alkali constituent of his glass batch. The result was a metal, heavier than Venetian glass, but with a 'brilliance and light dispersing quality unmatched by any previous manufacture'. In 1674, Ravenscroft became the official glassmaker to the Glass Sellers Company and continued to work at his Savoy Glass House and in an experimental factory at Henley-on-Thames until his death in 1681. His work was continued by an associate Hawley Bishopp. Ravenscroft called his development 'Flint Glass'—possibly because he was obtaining his silica from English flints rather than Venetian sands or stone. Ravenscroft was also concerned with the process of 'crizzling' which appeared on his glasses, in which the vessels were covered with minute cracks. He remedied the defect by 1676, and obtained permission to seal his best pieces with a raven's head, and many examples survive showing varying degrees of clarity in the metal (see Plates 14 and 15). This was the great encouragement to glassmaking in England, and very soon there were factories all over the country making remarkably fine glass, thus laying the foundation of the vast nineteenth-century industry.

The most important development for our concern which followed was the re-introduction towards the end of the seventeenth century by the Bohemians, of glass cutting and faceting. The art rapidly spread to Germany where the spectacular results quickly brought fame and a large export market. The first responses in England did not seem to be too enthusiastic, and it was not until the mid-eighteenth century that English cut glass began to appear more commonly. Little of the early cut glass survives as much old glass was destroyed for re-use following the rise in the cost of materials brought about by the introduction of excise duty on glass in 1745–6. Wheel engraving became popular with the 'flowered glasses' of the early 1740s, but the finest English and particularly Newcastle glasses decorated in this manner were worked abroad, especially in the Netherlands. Styles in cutting changed and proliferated with fashions during the eighteenth century. In the nineteenth century the taste for over-embellishment led to enormously complex cutting, culminating in a dazzling array of faceting styles on display at the Great Exhibition of 1851. So many fashions arose and disappeared in the nineteenth century, during which time almost every conceivable style in glassmaking was revived.

Bottles and Decanters

From the earliest times, man has been absorbed by the problem of making drinking vessels, and, subsequently, vessels for transporting, storing, and serving drinks. In the early years of their manufacture, bottles performed all three services, but gradually were developed especially for the first two categories. Out of the third developed the decanter. A wide variety of materials including leather, bone, many metals and pottery were used before and alongside glass, until around the mid-eighteenth century when glass began to take precedence over all materials for the serving, storing, and carrying of liquids. Glass bottles for holding liquid of one kind or another had been known from antiquity, and continued to be made down the centuries. From medieval times documents exist listing ownership of such things as 'a little bottel', or 'a glasse bottle'. In recent years bottles have received a considerable amount of study and an increasing number of collectors on both sides of the Atlantic confine their interest in glass to this particular variety.

In England glass bottles were still rather a novelty as late as the mid-seventeenth century. Until after that time Rhenish stoneware and Lambeth Delft pottery jugs were almost exclusively used to carry wine to the table. The white pottery Lambeth jugs usually bore initials, and sometimes the name of the wine—Claret, Whit (white wine), Sack, and more rarely Rhenish Wine. They bear dates from 1637–72. Stoneware bottles made of very highly fired clay were in plentiful supply until around 1653, but are noted to be very rare by the 1670s—glass had superseded. A few glass bottles survive which show a formal link with the early pottery jugs. In shape they are similar, and like the pottery jugs bear a handle and occasionally a seal. They are known as serving bottles. The Arms and Regulations of the Glass Sellers Company bear witness to the relationship between glass and pottery. The Arms show 'a Venetian glass cup between a laverpot [ewer] of white ware on the dexter', etc. The byelaws specify the manufacture along with glasses, of stone pots (stoneware) or earthenware bottles. There exists scant information about where bottles were being made between 1650–90. In 1662 a patent was granted to Henry Holder and John Colenet, as they claimed to have 'invented and brought unto perfection of making glass vessels' or bottles. They were permitted a fourteen-year licence provided that the bottles were suitable for containing full measures of liquids. These two had been making glass bottles as early as 1632 for Sir Kenelm Digby, a naval officer, diplomatist, and gentleman, called by some 'the ornament of England', but by John Evelyn, the more cynical diarist, 'a teller of strange things' and 'an arrant mountebank'. Two London glass dealers alleged, only one month after the patent was granted, that Henry Holder and partner had not been responsible for the 'invention' of bottles, rather that it had been Sir Kenelm Digby. Patent was withdrawn, but one wonders quite how gullible the authorities were, or were prepared to be, to believe either the accusers or the accused that such a basic commodity could be 'invented'. In 1696, John Haughton, Fellow of the Royal Society wrote *An account of all the glasshouses in England and Wales* listing their situation and 'the sorts of glass each house makes'. There were ninety listed, and Haughton pointed out that the majority were in

London and Bristol. Of the total, forty-two produced bottles, presumably sufficient for the home market, for he also notes that in 1694 no more than eight dozen bottles were imported into the country—'I presume their importation to have quite spoilt'. Haughton reveals the composition of bottle glass at the time; 'our green glass, or glass for bottles is made of any sort of ashes, well powdered, and ordinary sea sand from Woolwich, etc. This is at present what occurs on this subject . . . By another [informant] I understand they use kelp and pulverine, [sea weeds], which are still but a finer sort of potash.' It may be of interest here to quote also Lady Ruggles-Brise, perhaps the most admired writer on sealed and other bottles, in her note on the scientific analysis of the component parts of bottle glass: 'Silica 59 parts, Potash 3 parts, Lime 25 parts, Alumina 6 parts, and Oxide of Iron 7 parts'. With so many glass houses at work, it is to be expected that there was considerable variation in design. Each bottle was individually blown and the size of each finished object judged by eye. But experienced glassmakers, like potters, are soon able to achieve a uniformity of production should they choose. The bottles were blown from the gathering of glass at the end of the blowing rod at first as a round bubble. The base was then flattened on a marver and a pontil (or puntee which is an iron rod) attached to this flattened base. With the blowing rod removed the neck of the bottle was then reheated and worked and tooled, with a 'string rim' or trail of glass being added on the neck near the mouth, being provided in the first instance to retain the string which held the cork in place. (Later when the cork was driven flush with the top and stringing became unnecessary, the string rim remained but was raised level with the orifice.) After the neck was worked the pontil was pushed up before being snapped off, to enable the bottle to stand firmly. This 'kick' or 'kick-up' was necessary as not only if left would it make the bottle unsteady, but the rough mark would scratch the surface on which the bottle stood or was pushed around on while serving. Still it is not surprising that few bottles are quite alike, but by observing the gradual changes in shape which occurred, we can begin to chart a history of bottles. However, charting the history or sequence of bottle shapes is only a guide and one must take the precaution, unless the bottle is sealed, of adding *circa*.

Sealed Bottles

From 1650, or perhaps earlier, bottles were adorned on the shoulder with a glass seal, inscribed with a name, initials, sometimes an address, sometimes a date, a coat of arms, or a crest. A seal was a pad of glass—a drop of molten glass, impressed with a metal stamp cut in intaglio exactly as if it was to be used with sealing wax. The seal was of necessity applied while the bottle was just made and hot, otherwise cracking would take place if the two pieces were not to cool and contract at the same rate. There exist over eight hundred seals according to Lady Ruggles-Brise, and by the 1660s 'glass bottles were definitely the fashion, and sealed bottles, perhaps, the sign of a "great lord"' as much as of taste and position. Two of the earliest sealed English wine bottles known were found in London bearing the seal R.W. An identical seal was excavated in Jamestown, Virginia, the first permanent English settlement in the New World. One of the colonists in the first half of the seventeenth century was a man named Ralph Wormeley, upon whose property the seal R.W. was discovered. As he died in 1651 and the two London bottles are of the earliest known shape perhaps it can be supposed that they were made not later than 1651. There also exist proprietary seals, and factory seals. The former were borne by tavern and other bottles—the seal put on so that each man might retain his own property. Factory seals or merchants' marks were put on all kinds of glass to show from which factory the specimens had emanated, and could be interpreted as a guarantee of quality in the manner of a modern trade mark. The raven's head was the seal of the factory of Ravenscroft, and like the ancient workers of Sidon who also marked their wares, guaranteed the quality as well as identifying the maker.

It is possible to produce some rough groupings into which most bottles fall according to shape: The earliest group, made from 1630–85 have been called 'Shaft-and-Globe' for the body was spherical and the neck tall, perhaps influenced by the fashion for length and height at the time. They were most popular around 1650 (see Plates 2 and 3). The next development was noticeable by 1670 and was the shortening of the neck while the body remained bulbous. By 1680 the neck is so short as to render pouring difficult, and by 1690 the neck has become so shortened that the bottle is difficult to grip satisfactorily. There is a deep kick into a wide squat body. From 1715 and noticeably from 1725 the design of wine bottles has begun to change. The stumpy neck and bulbous body of the preceding thirty years declines and the outline becomes sharper. The shoulder slope is less pronounced and the body sides begin to follow a more straight line from shoulder to base (see Plate 4). The high kick remains. The well-defined shoulder and straight lines of the new type of bottle are the first indication of the development towards the wine bottle of today. The Methuen Treaty between Portugal and England was concluded in 1703 in which it was agreed that England should export wool in return for Portuguese wine being allowed in at lower duty than was being levied on French wine. Not surprisingly, Portuguese wines, and Port in particular, soon began to be more popular than French wines. With Port drinking, there arose the need for a container requiring a minimum of storage space which could be set aside in order for the wine to mature. A straight sided bottle proved the answer—it could be laid down without trouble and stored easily (see Plates 7 and 9). By 1740–41 bottles with longer necks and cylindrical bodies were evolving. This was a period of transition, notably with bottle sides becoming more vertical, but until 1778 bottles were often of wide dimension. Around 1741 bottles had a body which was squattish in profile with the neck and shoulder about the same height as the body, but by the last quarter of the century the bodies of bottles were mostly tall and slim (see Plates 10 and 11).

American readers may be interested to note that a great deal of useful and worthwhile information about the history of old English wine bottles has resulted from the careful archaeological investigations in the United States. The site of the former Jamestown in Virginia has yielded no fewer than 20,000 fragments of bottles from two digs spanning a number of years. Three complete bottles were recovered and 106 seals were found. The first colonists left London in 1606 and named 'Jamestowne' after their King. By 1642 the colony had grown from an original 105 souls to 8,000. Although it is known that there were attempts to start local glass houses, no bottles were made there, and it is accepted that all the excavated glass was made in England. The more successful of the colonists sent home for bottles, many of which they had ornamented fashionably with their marks in the form of seals. There are two seals of historical interest bearing the initials F N. They are thought by some authorities including Lady Ruggles-Brise, to have belonged to Sir Francis Nicholson who was Lieutenant-Governor of Virginia between 1690 and 1705. He recommended the removal, after civil disturbances, of the seat of government from Jamestown to Middle Plantation—then the name for Williamsburg. This information thus would date the seals to the last quarter of the seventeenth century.

The practice of private sealing continued throughout the eighteenth century, and at the same time wine merchants and tavern keepers did the same, in part to insure that their bottles were not used by competitors and in part as an advertisement. By the time Victoria was on the throne such sealed marks were becoming rare and soon afterwards they were more or less past history, the process of moulding on bottles having to some measure taken over. Of the moulding process we have a description from 1852 which tells how a man blew the body of the bottle into a mould (presumably made of wood or metal and hinged), where it received the intended shape, included in which was often the glass house or merchant's name. The mould was removed, a pontil attached, the blowing iron knocked off and the bottle reheated at the furnace so that the neck could be worked. During the nineteenth century the Bristol and London bottle makers faced increasing competition from the north of England where both fuel and labour were more plentiful, and the death blow was struck with the development by 1900 of machines which could outstrip any craftsman, producing an almost endless supply of bottles.

Corks, Corkscrews and Binning

Perhaps we could here allow ourselves a small digression into a mention of corks, corkscrews, and binning. The necks of bottles were closed with various substances such as beeswax or leather tied down with string as early as Egyptian and Roman times, but it was not until the eighteenth century that stoppers made of cork bark began to be used widely. They were developed largely because of the practice of allowing wine to mature in the bottle. The best corks came from Spain. The longer the wine was required to mature the longer the cork, and the softer the substance the larger the cork must be. From the earliest years of the seventeenth century there are mentions of corks. In the accounts dated 1605 of the butler to the Lords of the Star Chamber there is a mention of an expenditure of two shillings and six pence for 'corks to stop bottles'. We are so familiar as to take for granted the 'spirally shaped instrument for drawing corks from bottles', and as with the invention of glass blowing there is no man recorded to whom the invention can be ascribed. It would seem inappropriate to go into a history of corkscrews save to say that they developed from simple metal screws with a ring on the end into the enormously complicated machines some of us find so difficult to use today. As mentioned before, the practice of allowing wines to mature in the bottle began to be widespread around the 1730s and 1740s, and the term referring to the storage of these bottles was 'binning'. The squat bulbous shape of the early bottles was not convenient for storing them on their sides, for otherwise the wine could not remain in contact with the cork and by keeping it moist, swollen and airtight. If the cork shrank air would get to the wine and encourage fungi which would spoil the wine by creating vinegar. Thus a bottle had to be devised which would both stand up for use and inspection, and also easily lie on its side for storage and economy of space. It is, however, thought that some of the earliest binned bottles were stored upside down as there are examples with traces of wine sediment remaining in the neck of the bottle.

The collecting of sealed and other bottles can be a most enjoyable and absorbing pleasure, for apart from the fun of searching out examples which are characteristic of certain periods there is always the chance that one will find a treasure, and the possibility of detective work in tracing seals to discover their owners and origins. Also bottles travelled so far that one can find them in the most unexpected corners.

Decanters

Rather in the way that bottles developed, the evolution of decanters was also an orderly process and with no great variety until the end of the eighteenth century and the early part of the nineteenth, and even then variety was more a matter of ornament. Originally, to decant meant to pour liquid from one vessel to another leaving behind sediment. The pouring of liquid into any vessel was done by tilting or 'canting' the container. By the end of the seventeenth century, decanting had come to mean pouring from a storage vessel, most usually a cask, into some kind of bottle for serving at table, and bottles made especially for this purpose came to be called decanters. The dark coloured wine bottle had been functional for serving and storing wine, but decorative serving vessels were demanded, and this demand created new scope for the glassmakers.

The earliest decanters, made by George Ravenscroft in the late-seventeenth century, were called by him 'bottles'. They were made in the expensive glass-of-lead, and their ornamentation indicated that they were intended to be decorative as well as useful. The sort of decorations are discussed in relation to Plates 14 and 15, but all the features and combinations of ornament were reminiscent of Venetian styles. There are two main types of late-seventeenth century decanter. One type had an almost cylindrical body, sloping slightly inwards towards the base, with curved shoulders, and a short cylindrical neck with a wide pouring mouth pinched into a spout on one side. The enlarged mouth facilitated decanting either from a domestic cask or a vintners bottle without the use of a pouring funnel. This type was almost always provided with a handle. (See Plates 14 and 15.) The second type of decanter was slightly similar to a modern chianti bottle, and followed the shaft-and-globe shape of contemporary wine bottles. Although Ravenscroft states that his decanters were provided with stoppers, the string rim for securing corks which appeared on wine bottles was a feature of these vessels. Some shaft-and-globe decanters rested on a rim foot, or like ordinary bottles were without a separate foot. The rim foot did not last longer than the first quarter of the eighteenth century. These early decanters of both types reflect the simple bold shapes of the Baroque style culminating in the simplicity of the Queen Anne style with the feeling of height and volume. We must remember that the word 'decanter' probably came into use in the last decade of the seventeenth century and was at first used in relation to the pottery Lambeth Delft Jugs, and that it has been employed retrospectively to describe the work of Ravenscroft who died in 1681.

At the turn of the century the shaft-and-globe shape continued, providing a basis of decanter shapes extending over our entire period of interest. The glassmakers deliberately made the early decanters of better quality glass and better ornamented to give them importance and no doubt stimulate the market. In 1710 an advertisement in *The Tatler* included amongst wares offered for sale 'all sorts of decanters', but examples are rare, and few exist without handles. In the 1720s a mallet-shaped decanter began to emerge. These were named so because they were like a mason's or sculptor's mallet (see Plate 17). There are minor variations to be seen, but these decanters retain a strong family likeness. The necks vary in length, but are never shorter than the bodies. The outline is rectangular with sides straight, or very slightly sloping either way. There is a kick-up on the base and no ring foot. We can distinguish three rough types:

1. Bodies of normal circular section, this kind sometimes having a handle.
2. Bodies with six or more sides sometimes with a handle and spout.
3. Four-lobed bodies of cruciform section as shown in Plate 16. This type was more common after 1730 and was of functional shape, and remained current until the reign of George III.

Judging from the numbers which have survived, these cruciform decanters were popular, although full bottle size examples are becoming increasingly difficult to find. The mallet shaped decanters retained their neck rings until about 1745. In that decade mallet shaped decanters began to change, and appeared with an increased height coupled with an increased downward slope of the shoulders. This type with its new profile became known and advertised as the Shouldered Decanter. After 1745 the lip became turned outward and flattened and within twenty years this feature was common to almost all decanters (see Plate 20). The lip was no longer related to the string rim but facilitated pouring without dribbling. The kind of stopper associated with the shouldered decanter was of spire form, and a fair quantity of them survive together. Shoulders and sides departing from the vertical by turning either inwards or outwards became popular from the mid-century and formed the basis of many subsequent styles.

Most decanters of this early period were plain, and there was a vogue for rounded plain decanters of heavy metal and fitted round stoppers. As wheel cutting on glass was becoming popular it was not long before decanters came to be decorated in this manner. Cutting on the glasses was somewhat tentative at first, no doubt partly due to inexperience but also the Excise Act had encouraged the making of thin walled decanters and vessels. The earliest all-over pattern was the shallow diamond faceting used on the stems of certain wine glasses and which was developed between 1745–70. The simplicity and shallowness of the cutting served to enhance the contents of the bottle and faceted glass soon became popular (see Plate 18). Hexagonal facets appeared next, but were rarely used for all-over cutting, and appeared more often on necks and shoulders in association with decorative cutting, in particular festoons and stars. Scale cutting was used from 1760 as with drinking glasses, but again it seems to have been confined to the lower necks and shoulders of decanters. As the process was laborious, broader cutting wheels were employed resulting in larger scales and a bolder effect (see Plate 20). A single or multiple circuit of diamonds in a band around the centre of the body was a pattern which originated and became most popular and fashionable during the Regency (see Plates 30 and 44).

In the middle of the eighteenth century enamelling on glass was revived and became very popular, and mention must be made of the remarkable and beautiful work of brother and sister William and Mary Beilby. Most of their work was done in a bluish- or pinkish-white monochrome, in designs in a vivacious rococo style including motifs such as landscapes with obelisks and ruins, growing vines, scrollwork, and depictions of rural pastimes. Their first designs were executed about 1762 and they continued working until 1778. They decorated decanters, and there exist signed examples marked 'Beilby inv & pinx'.

Perhaps we should here note something about the techniques of cutting and faceting. As mentioned in the introduction, the use of a wheel for cutting lines and facets goes back to the very early days of blown glass. There are basically four operations once the thick blank or object to be cut has been prepared. These are marking, roughing, smoothing, and polishing. The first is the painting of a sketch of the required design on to the glass with a mixture of red lead and turpentine. Once this has been done, the roughing operation is carried out with the design being marked out by means of a revolving wheel of iron, about 18 inches in diameter, which has an edge chosen to suit the particular shape of cut. The cutting edge of the wheel is fed with a fine stream of wet sand, and it is this abrasive which acts when the vessel is pressed firmly against the revolving wheel and serves to cut into the surface. This leaves a coarse frost-like finish, which is then smoothed on sandstone wheels of lessening coarseness, with finer cuts and lines being added. It is here that a keen eye for outline and accuracy, and an ability to execute regular geometric designs is of paramount importance, for the slightest slip can spoil the design.

The making of coloured glass is also a technique requiring great skill if the colours are to be even and controlled. Coloured glass has been admired and sought after since the beginning of glassmaking, and in England the finest coloured glass was first made in the eighteenth and early-nineteenth centuries. There were many country wares of the Nailsea type (see Plate 50—commentary), where the colours were largely uncontrolled but vessels made in perfectly produced and controlled blues, greens, and purples can be seen in Plates 23, 26, and 32. The colours were produced by adding mineral colouring agents to the mixture of raw materials. The term 'Bristol Blue' originated in this context, as smalt, pulverized cobalt, was imported from Saxony into Bristol, and glassmakers were obliged to go there to obtain this colouring agent. The main colouring agents were: cobalt and copper for blue, iron, copper, and chromium for green, manganese and nickel for violet, and arsenic, tin, fluorspar, calcium, and phosphate for 'white opal'. It was in the mid-nineteenth century that coloured glass acquired enormous popularity (see Plates

49 and 58) largely as a result of the importation of Bohemian coloured wares. The period from 1780 to 1800 is perhaps the most important for decanters, for it is the beginning of the Anglo-Irish glass era. Naturally, Irish manufacturers made many types of glass wares apart from decanters, but the latter were the most characteristic and probably the best known. The Glass Excise Act of 1745 imposed no tax on the Irish industry, but it forbade the importation of anything other than English glass into Ireland, and prohibited the export from Ireland of any kind of glass. Thus it is not very surprising that Irish glassmaking was not a flourishing industry. But in 1780 the export ban was removed, and the consequences were far reaching. One of the most important centres was Belfast. A Bristol glassmaker named Benjamin Edwards had already set up a glass house in the late 1770s, and with the aid of an English cutter, was able to supply the local markets. In 1781, being free of the pernicious English taxes and the export ban, Edwards expanded and he began to advertise plain and cut decanters. Most Belfast decanters of the late-eighteenth century were of tapering form, which was a form which developed from the late 1760s onwards, in which the shoulders almost disappeared altogether resulting in a soft outline indenting towards the base. Belfast decanters particularly emphasized the degree of curvature in the profile. Their lower parts were embellished either with a circuit of wheel-cut comb fluting (called so from a fancied resemblance to the teeth of a comb) which occur on free-blown examples, or moulded flutes on others. The latter decoration was made during the blowing operation while the metal was plastic. Shallow wooden or metal moulds were prepared with slight vertical ribs all round the inside, and sometimes the name of a factory in a circle on the bottom, and then the balloon of soft glass was inflated into the mould. These moulded flutes were sometimes overcut. Moulded basal flutes were by no means exclusive to Belfast, and were common on a vast number of decanters produced in many Bristol and Irish houses (see Plates 31 and 33). Cut decoration was far less emphasized on Belfast decanters, but neck rings which became a common feature on decanters and which were not only decorative, but served to ensure a safe grip, are useful in identifying Belfast decanters. On most Belfast vessels the neck rings were two in number instead of the usual three found elsewhere, and were triangular in section, and also the lip rings project only very slightly, sometimes less than the neck rings. Stoppers remained the simple flat vertical type either of bevelled pear shape, or a flat disc with a circular boss in the middle, the so-called bull's eye. The other most important Irish glass houses were situated in Cork, Dublin, and Waterford (see Plates 29 and 33). The Waterford glass has become surrounded in myth, with almost magical qualities attributed to the metal, and the name being attached to a vessel resulting in a considerable increase in the price. The most important glass house in Waterford was set up by two Irish merchants called Penrose, to make 'plain and flint glasses'. The firm was associated with and managed by an Englishman, John Hill of Stourbridge, who brought glassmakers and cutters from England, and produced Stourbridge designs. By clever advertising, maintaining a very high standard of production, and a good export market which included America, the company flourished and continued until 1851 (see Plate 38). From 1830 onwards the styles of cut-glass were recorded by the foreman cutter at the

Waterford works, and it is possible to see the development of decanters into more heavy shapes (see Plates 47 and 48), with 'Gothic' patterns, and a revival of the globular shape and its variations (see Plate 54). Cutting remained popular, and the repeal of the glass excise in 1845 encouraged the production of thicker vessels thus allowing for deeper and more elaborate cutting which culminated in the vast and dazzling displays of the Great Exhibition of 1851.

Glassmaking in the nineteenth century was influenced by the development of many new techniques, and characterized by the revival of almost every style that had existed. Most of the revivals were very short lived. But new developments such as lustres were taken up and brought to the most luxurious climaxes in the products of Louis Comfort Tiffany in America. The growth of enthusiasm for coloured glass around the middle of the century encouraged the production of a great number and wide variety of scent and toilet bottles. The first glass vessels ever to exist were used to contain scent, and there have been few periods since then when scent has not been associated with glass containers. The first most important vogue in England was about 1780–90 when there were made charming coloured and gilt examples with beautiful faceting and gold tops (see Plate 55). The 1860 to 1900 boom in coloured glass produced many scent bottles, of which two types were the most usual, the clear faceted examples and the frosted cameo cut glasses. Around 1860, double compartment scent bottles were popular, in various colours such as blue, apple green, opaline green cut with 'windows', and red. The dividing partition was in the centre, and there was a silver top containing a tiny glass stopper at each end, these tiny vessels being no more than four to five inches in length. Amongst the fashions for revivals at this period, cameo work, such as was first practised by the Romans, became popular. The focus of the revival was a vase painstakingly made by a Stourbridge worker, who in his spare time took up the challenge from a local glassmaker to copy the Portland Vase. The vase occupied John Northwood for three years, and after cracking in two and being finally completed, it joined the original in the British Museum. The success of the copy led some Stourbridge makers, notably Webb and Richardson, to market pieces made in the cameo technique. The long and complicated processes were speeded up by the use of acids and mechanical carving tools, although the final work had to be done by hand. The larger and more complicated pieces took many years and cost a great deal, but the smaller and less costly examples are perhaps the best known (see Plate 59).

In trying to cover such an enormous field, it is certain that there will be many gaps and omissions, partly due to lack of space and personal preference. However, hopefully, the range of glasses selected will please and interest those who may wish to begin collecting within this field, as well as encourage and inform confirmed collectors. A minimum number of museum pieces has been included in our selection, in order to illustrate the sort of vessels which are available on the market.

I would like to thank all those friends and colleagues who have so kindly loaned pieces for illustration, and the photographer for his friendly assistance and his beautiful presentation of each item. My particular thanks must also go to my wife Joan for her patience during many long evenings of writing.

2 Onion-shape Sealed Bottle

This bottle, 7½″ high, sealed B Y D D E R - B O O N T H I S T L E and dated 1674, although it has no recorded history, is regarded as one of the rarest to have survived bearing a date and an unusual name. The glass is of typical 'bottle' quality, containing a number of air bubbles and streaks resembling cracks and which are often wrongly described as such. The crest in the middle of the seal is rather indistinct. The early bottles of this squat shape were used both for storing before binning became current, and for serving purposes as semi-decanters. Were there no identifying marks on the bottle, the shape would certainly give us a clue to the approximate dating for it is a characteristic example of the Shaft-and-Globe bottle produced between 1630 and 1685.

3 Tavern and Private Seals

The squat-shaped bottle (above) is sealed with the coat-of-arms of the Three Tuns tavern in Oxford, and is dated 1713. It is approximately 6″ tall. The earliest known dated tavern bottle is sealed R M P 1657, although there exist undated bottles which are quite possibly earlier. Many of the earliest bottles have been excavated in the oldest part of Oxford, and mostly bear the names or insignia of five taverns: the Salutation, the Mermaid, the Crown, the Three Tuns, and the Kings Head. University and city records have given us the history of the Three Tuns. It was first owned 1639–60 by Humphrey Bodicot, and then from 1666–71 by Richard and Elizabeth Port, the latter continuing in possession until 1687. Her servants, George Brown and Joane Richardson, married and were licensees from ?1689–93. Then came William and Ann Taylor 1693–5, and after that Culpeper and Ann Tomlinson 1697–1712; thereafter Ann Tomlinson, widow, continued until 1719, and was thus the owner of the tavern when this bottle was made.

The private bottle (below) is sealed with a crest bearing the head of a unicorn with its neck pierced by an arrow, and is inscribed 'Robert Hughes' for the owner and dated 1733. It is 7″ tall. Armorial bearings as on this bottle can frequently be as useful a guide to the date of manufacture as dated seals, for it can be possible to trace the latest date at which a certain coat was born.

Richard Dennis

4 Early Cut Glass Bottle

Glass was not only used in combination
with silver for cruet stands but also for
spirit bottles and flasks which could be
easily carried when travelling. This example, as with the decanter illustrated in
Plate 18, shows the earliest type of English cutting—simple facet design, and it
is possible that this example is a little
earlier. The first recorded advertisement
of English cut glass was by John Ackerman in 1719, who declared that 'John
Ackerman, at the Rose and Crown,
Cornhill, continues to sell all sorts of
tea, chinaware, plain and diamond cut
flint glasses, white stoneware, etc.'. The
silver cup fitting on to the base of the
bottle is engraved with a family coat of
arms on each side, and underneath the
silver hinged lid is a tiny glass stopper.
The silver maker is identified in Sir
Charles Jackson's *English Goldsmiths
and their Marks*, as G.M., whose mark is
recorded from a toy tankard of 1697.
The arms, as displayed on the silver cup
are for Edgar Devereux, Esq., of the Red
House, Ipswich, Suffolk, who married
Temperance, daughter of Robert Spar-
row of Wickham Brook, September
1681.

S. J. Shrubsole Ltd

5 Double Wine Bottle

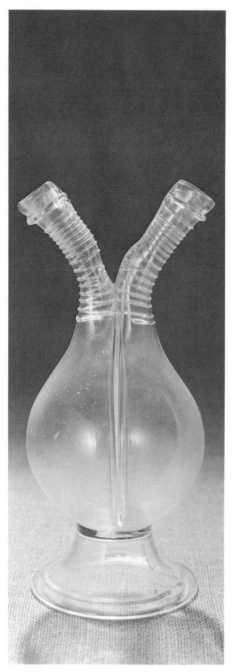

This is an amusing though not uncommon double wine bottle made by blowing two bubbles of glass about the same size and shape and then bringing the two together and reheating so that the central partition of two membranes should be properly joined. The foot would then have been added before the glass was transferred to a pontil so that the necks of the joined vessels could be ornamented and drawn in alternate directions. There exist examples decorated with engraving which names the contents; not uncommonly 'Red Port' and 'White Port'. The flared base has a folded rim. This double thickness of glass was intended to strengthen the foot against constant use. It measures 9″ high and would be dated about 1740.

Cecil Davis Ltd

6 Small Engraved Bottles

The two outside bottles are engraved 'OIL' (left) and 'VINEGAR' (right) and are related to the engraved label decanter series (see Plate 17). The oil bottle is mallet shaped and has a flat facet-cut stopper and the vinegar bottle a flat plain stopper. The small decanter in the centre is engraved with a growing vine pattern and has a triple plain-ringed neck and moulded mushroom stopper. A collection of this kind of small bottle or decanter can represent a very wide variety of types, styles, and sizes, for they were produced in many variations. In order, left, right, and centre, the three bottles illustrate the diminution of the high kick of early bottles becoming less pronounced towards the end of the eighteenth century, until the kick eventually disappeared and the scar left by the removal of the puntee was ground smooth, a practice which has continued since the early-nineteenth century until now. The height of all three bottles is about 7″.

27

7 Brown Sealed Wine Bottle

This early bottle bears in its seal only the initials W R and the date 1752. It also shows a variation in shape as it is taller than earlier bottles and its sides are almost straight. It is about 8″ high. As we have already noted, the Methuen Treaty of 1703 between England and Portugal permitted Portuguese wines into England at an import duty somewhat below that placed on French wines. Human nature being as it is, it is not surprising to note that Portuguese wines soon outstripped French wines in popularity. However the taste for matured wines, particularly Port, soon produced a need for a method of storing wines so that they could mature. Thus binning evolved, and the cylindrical bottle was developed as a storage container which needed only a minimum of space.

8 Straight Sided Bottle

This bottle is inscribed 'Dommet Junior, Offwell' and is dated 1777. Despite its later date and straight sides, this bottle was probably not made for binning as its circumference is rather too wide. It has a capacity of nearly two modern bottles and a height of 8″. Lady Ruggles-Brise in her main list of sealed bottles mentions a bottle sealed 'E. Dommett Junr' 1774, and it is possible that the two may have belonged to the same owner, the content of the seal being changed only slightly perhaps to indicate a move, or change of bottle maker. The dark colour of these bottles was such largely because demand was great and this type of impure metal could be made cheaply. Also storing wine in dark bottles was thought to protect it from daylight.

Richard Dennis

9 University Sealed Bottle

The seal on this cylindrical bottle bears the initials A.S.C.R. standing for All Souls Common Room, Oxford. Although the seals carried the initials of university common rooms, the bottles are believed to have been the property of the owner of the inn which supplied them, or of the wine merchants, and not of the colleges themselves. The bottle is *c.* 11″ tall and would be dated *c.* 1790. One of the earliest of these university sealed bottles is dated 1744, and the latest examples continue well into the nineteenth century. Bottles with university seals (both Oxford and Cambridge), are readily available today, as their popularity at the colleges encouraged the production of large numbers. The most usual examples bear the seals of Emmanuel College, All Souls Common Room (initials, as above), and Selwyn College. Lincoln College, St. John's College and Magdalen College are all rather rare now. City of London names are occasionally found, for example, Inner Temple and Middle Temple.

Cecil Davis Ltd

10 Sealed Wine Bottle

This bottle is sealed John Croad Esq., Keyham, and dated 1797. This example also shows one of the early types of narrow cylindrical bottles, made after binning became the fashion for storing wine. (See page 29.) Height: *c*. 12″.

Richard Dennis

11 Large Sealed Bottle

The seal is inscribed R.C. 1811 and is an example of the bottles on which initials only were put on the seal. The shape of the bottle is interesting because, in spite of its later date, it does not conform to the usual dimensions of bottles made for binning. (See Plate 7.) It is 12″ tall.

Richard Dennis

Cecil Davis Ltd

12 Pair of Condiment Bottles

These bottles are beautifully cut with a sunray pattern of step flutes, with broad flutes above and they are of the finest quality. They have oval pedestal bases which are also flute cut. The silver hallmarked tops are not pierced and were, therefore, intended for oil and vinegar. Height *c.* $6\frac{1}{2}''$; date *c.* 1815.

The oval shape is unusual and the bottles were probably not, therefore, intended to fit into a silver stand. These stands usually held circular bottles for oil and vinegar, the larger ones also being fitted for salt cellar, mustard pot and sugar castor. Some oil and vinegar bottles were made to take silver or Sheffield plated mounts and handles; small glass stoppers were also fitted. Most silver makers made provision for placing stoppers in specially made rings between the larger ones in the stand, for when the bottles were in use.

Cannon Hall Art Gallery, Barnsley

13 Victorian Fire Extinguisher

These rare items were manufactured for the London and other fire brigades, and placed in hotels, clubs, shops and public rooms. Made in moulds, they were marked in moulded letters 'The Imperial Grenade' in a circle simulating a strap and buckle. In the centre was the wording 'Fire Extinguisher', and this was surmounted by the Prince of Wales' feathers as a form of decoration. They were intended to be hurled at the centre of the blaze and although fairly limited in use, they were effective. The contents when the bottle was broken let off the equivalent of carbolic acid gas, and the grenade could be described as the forerunner of our present chemical extinguishers. Usually kept in wire cages for two, they were generally made in a variety of colours, such as greens, browns and deep blues. Height: $6\frac{1}{4}''$; date: *c.* 1860.

14 Ravenscroft Style Jug

This late-seventeenth-century claret jug illustrates the great achievements made possible for glassmakers by Ravenscroft's development of lead glass. The addition of oxide of lead to the glass batches produced a much stronger and better quality glass. It shows no sign of crizzling which occurred in some of his early pieces and consisted of a mass of tiny cracks all over the surface of the glass. The glass can only be attributed to Ravenscroft, for, while being stylistically close to recognized pieces it does not bear his seal. It is decorated with applied chain trailing, a vermiform collar, and pronounced vertical gadrooning from the base. The plain handle is applied, and the stopper is of the loose-fitting type, decorated with close deep-moulded flutes. As the drink for which this decanter jug was intended was carried from the cask to the table and most likely consumed entirely, there was no reason for the stoppers to be made in such a way as to prevent evaporation. In Ravenscroft's advertisements the decanters, or bottles as he called them, were said always to be accompanied by stoppers. However the fact that the stoppers were quite loose fitting and served no purpose other than decoration resulted in a great number being discarded or lost. Thus any vessel complete with stopper, such as the one illustrated, must be considered a great rarity. Height: $11\frac{1}{4}''$; date: *c.* 1680.

15 Ravenscroft Claret Jug

This jug is similar to the vessel illustrated in Plate 14, with some slight stylistic variations. There is a more elaborate sealed example in the British Museum decorated with 'nipt diamond waies' decoration, and there are other attributable or sealed Ravenscroft products in the Victoria and Albert Museum London and the Ashmolean Museum in Oxford bearing this decoration. Height: 9″; date: *c*. 1680. The nipt diamond waies decoration was one of a fairly limited number of motifs employed by Ravenscroft and other seventeenth-century glassmakers to decorate their wares. The decorations of gadrooning or ribbing, the chain-like motif as seen on the shoulder of this example and on the body of the preceding jug, and the nipt diamond decorations go back as far as the Roman period and may be seen on Roman Syrian glasses of the second to fourth centuries A.D. A logical suggestion has been advanced concerning the origin of the term 'nipt diamond waies' and would seem to be reasonable, that ribbing on the body of the vessel would be 'nipped diamond-wise' by a pincer-like tool, thus producing this decoration.

London Museum

35

16 Cruciform Decanter

These decanters, although sometimes considered as not being particularly elegant, nevertheless represent an important stage in the development of wine containers. They form an important link between the general use of green bottles and clear glass decanters. The term cruciform is self-explanatory, but the reason for making them in this shape was dictated by the fashion which prevailed at the time for drinking all wines cool or cold. By deeply indenting the body of the decanter and thus allowing the liquid a distribution where no part was far from the sides of the vessel, it was possible to cool the wine more easily. The decanter was usually placed in a bowl of water to cool, with glasses as well being cooled in large silver or ceramic bowls filled with water or ice. These decanters became very popular and were used extensively as, being made of thick metal, they stood up well to constant handling. Made in both pint and quart capacities they retained the collar at the top of the neck more for gripping than for stringing a cork since they were merely filled from the cellar and then used as a serving bottle at the table. The shape developed later into more of a mallet shape with indentations. Height: 7″; date: *c.* 1730.

Cannon Hall Art Gallery, Barnsley

17 Engraved Label Decanter

An elegant mallet-shaped decanter, engraved with a wine label 'Madeira', with a single collar at the top and pear shaped bull's eye stopper. Height: 11″; date: *c.* 1750. From the early-eighteenth century, silversmiths had been making engraved bottle tickets which were hung around the necks of plain decanters by thin chains. Bottles engraved with representations of these tickets appeared around 1755. In that year a Norwich dealer advertised in the *Norwich Mercury* 'new fashioned decanters with inscriptions engraved on them, Port, Claret, Mountain . . . decorated with vine leaves, grapes, etc.'. Within a few years the fashion was general. It is not easy to present a list in order of rarity, but it is roughly as follows: Champagne (still a red wine from the district, more in favour then than the sparkling white type), Jamaica Rum, Marsala, Florys, Mountain, Greek Wine, Ale, Cider, Sack, Red Wine, R. Wine, Beer, Burgundy, Hock, Lisbon, Lisboa, Claret, White and W. Wine, Port, and Madeira. On all examples the simulated chain extended round the shoulder. The accompanying engraved motifs varied considerably according to the contents for which the decanters were intended, but most usually they are variations on the vine design, hops and barley sprays, and conventional floral motifs.

Cannon Hall Art Gallery, Barnsley

18 Facet Cut Decanter

This quart size decanter illustrates the earliest English cutting which took the form of facets over the whole surface of the decanter, and the stopper cut to match. It was the forerunner of the more heavily cut decanters after 1800 and represented an important stage in the art of cutting in England. Height: *c.* 12″; date: *c.* 1750.

Thomas Betts established a business as a glass cutter at the King's Arms Shop, Charing Cross, shortly after 1738, and must surely have been one of the English pioneers of this craft. His trade card read: 'Makes and sells all sorts of curious cut Glass such as Cruets, Castors, Salts, Lustres, Dishes, Plates, Punch Bowles, Cream Bowles with Globes for Lanthorns, Large Salvers or Plates in Flint Glass or Looking Glass to fit China Dishes or without. Likewise curious work in Looking Glass either old or new in General. Cheaper and Better than hitherto has been done. He being the Real workman, for many Years'.

Obviously cut glass was produced in large quantities quite early in the eighteenth century and it is regrettable that not more has survived. The Glass Excise Act of 1745 imposed a duty on the raw materials used in glassmaking and probably much of the earlier glass which had become out of fashion was destroyed and resold as cullet (broken glass at the furnaces). This was because the Act allowed the glassmaker a certain amount of glass which could be remelted free of duty.

J. F. King

Derek C. Davis

19 Georgian Miniatures

Left to right:
  Rounded decanter with unusual engraved squares, single ringed neck. *c.* 1800
  Decanter of perfect proportions and quality decorated with broad and narrow flute cutting, double ringed neck, mushroom stopper. *c.* 1810
  Plain decanter with double ringed neck and mushroom stopper. *c.* 1800
  Plain decanter with unusual applied 'snake' neck in spiral design, and with mushroom stopper. *c.* 1790
  Cone-shaped Georgian ship's decanter, with ball shaped stopper. *c.* 1790
  Early facet cut decanter of mallet shape with faceted pinnacle stopper. *c.* 1760
  Heights: $3\frac{1}{2}''$ to $5\frac{1}{2}''$

Miniature examples of decanters such as these could have been made by apprentices either during their apprenticeship or as examples of their abilities and eligibility to become master workmen. There was a fashion in the seventeenth and eighteenth centuries which continued into the early-nineteenth century for furniture manufacturers to prepare miniature versions of suites of furniture ordered by clients in order to save considerable expense and labour should there be modifications which the would-be purchasers might require. It may possibly be that these decanters were intended for a similar use in advising retailers of the sort of goods available.

39

20 Georgian Quart Decanter

A fine Georgian quart size decanter, decorated with a central band of flat diamond cutting with broad flutes above and below; triple faceted ringed neck, bull's eye stopper. Height 11"; date *c.* 1810. This is a good example of the simple style of cutting which preceded the Regency age of brilliance and exuberance. The lightness and delicacy of ornament of the decanters of the 1780s and 90s has been replaced by the more solid and serious feeling of the later phase of Neo-Classicism. The following illustrations show the development up to Regency times and the subsequent heaviness and lack of elegant taste, with few exceptions, of the Victorian era. The transformation is shown very clearly in the type of cutting and the areas of the item covered.

Cecil Davis Ltd

Derek C. Davis

21   Group of Miniature Decanters

Although they cannot be considered common, it is surprising how many Georgian decanters in miniature and correct in every detail can be found, sometimes quite unexpectedly in auction rooms and antique shops. As mentioned in relation to the group illustrated in Plate 19, it is possible that they were intended to be made as direct prototypes and shown to clients or traders as what we might call today 'travellers' samples'. Of the several different types in this illustration, the details from left to right are:

Straight sided decanter decorated with broad flute cutting, triple ringed neck, flat cut stopper. Date: *c.* 1830

Pair of bottle-shaped decanters, the shoulders cut with flutes, plain circular stoppers. Date: *c.* 1810

Plain club-shaped decanter, kick-in base, bull's eye stopper. Date: *c.* 1790

Plain mallet-shaped decanter, circular flat stopper. Date: *c.* 1790

Pair of rare bottle-shaped decanters, decorated with vertical moulding, pear-shaped stoppers. Date: *c.* 1790

Plain mallet-shaped decanter, triple ringed neck, circular flat plain stopper. Date: *c.* 1790

Heights: $3\frac{1}{4}''$ to $5\frac{3}{4}''$

22 Three Plain Georgian Decanters

A pair of plain pint size Georgian decanters with triple ringed necks, and another of quart size. Heights: *c.* 8½″ and 9½″; date: *c.* 1790. The mid- and later-eighteenth-century vogue for plain glasses was at first perhaps an economically dictated taste caused by the tax on glass and the added expense of decoration. However quite possibly the particular clarity and attractiveness of the metal was a characteristic which strongly influenced the vogue. This quality is perhaps one of the main reasons for the present day popularity of plain eighteenth-century glass, and the enhancing effect of wine has encouraged collectors to continue to put them to practical use. These decanters and the following sequence illustrating decoration by engraving, moulding, and cutting are still obtainable at advantageous prices. This type of decanter was very much reproduced in the early years of this century, although almost without exception for no dishonest intention. The scratching and marking on the bases of the decanters through age and use make the modern pieces sometimes a little difficult to distinguish from their prototypes. However with a little experience it should not be difficult to recognize these later productions, not only by 'feel' but by the colour and character of the metal. Decanters very closely following this form are still being made and display as many attractive qualities as their older relatives.

Richard Dennis

23 Bristol Blue Quart Size Decanters

This fine pair of decanters made in 'Bristol Blue' glass is decorated with typical gilt name labels inscribed Brandy and Rum. Height: 10″. Date: *c.* 1790. This pair is in a particularly fine state of preservation as so often bottles are found with the gilding partially or completely rubbed away through constant handling, or else they are fitted with the wrong stoppers. The two main stopper shapes were pear and ball. There were numerous variations in the labels. Some were gilded with additional urn motifs as here, and others were embellished with bunches of grapes, heads of reindeers and simulated chains. Occasionally, tiny gilded corresponding numbers are found on the bases of the stoppers and underneath the decanters. In very rare instances, one or more of a set are signed by the Bristol glassmaker Isaac Jacobs. He also signed coloured glass finger bowls and plates.

43

24 Engraved Port Decanter

(*left*)

This is a typical port decanter of the late-eighteenth century, on which the wheel engraving has been executed particularly well with much attention having been paid to the details of the grape leaves and fruit. The plain triple rings on the neck follow the fashion of that time as does the moulded mushroom stopper. Examples of this type of decanter are not very difficult to find and can still be obtained at fairly reasonable prices. The general effect of the engraved design is much enhanced and accentuated when the decanter is filled with a dark red wine. The engraved motif of the growing vine was a pattern frequently adopted by the English artists, and it continued to be used on drinking glasses, decanters and finger bowls throughout the nineteenth century. For present day guidance, if the decanter is to be used, a Georgian quart size decanter holds more than a bottle of wine or sherry. Height: *c.* 11″; date: *c.* 1790.

Cecil Davis Ltd

Cecil Davis Ltd

25 Plain Georgian Magnum

A fine decanter holding two bottles of wine with triple ringed neck and flat stopper. Height: 12″; date: *c.* 1790. The pint and quart size decanters have already been considered in Plates 20 and 22, but as shown by the above example, even larger ones were made, although, by comparison with the smaller types, very few have survived. These were known by Biblical names and were as follows: Nebuchadnezzar, 20 bottles; Balthasor, 16 bottles; Salmanazar, 12 bottles; Methuselah, 8 bottles; Rehoboam, 6 bottles; Jeroboam, 4 bottles. The study of decanters can serve as an easy and useful guide to the dating of other table glass, especially from the types of cutting which were constantly changing and developing. The largest decanter recorded, with a capacity of 21 bottles was owned by the late Andre Simon and was exhibited at the Wine Trade Festival.

45

C. R. Butterworth

26 Bristol Green Pint Decanter

The colour most usually associated with products from the Bristol factories is blue, but green metal was quite often used. The illustration shows a plain green decanter of pint size, with triple ringed neck and bull's eye stopper. Blue and green examples of both quart and pint size were usually made with gilt labels (see opposite) naming the contents, but plain blue, green, and amethyst table glass is quite often to be found mentioned in the glassmakers' lists. Height: c. 7"; date: c. 1790.

27 Irish Flute Cut Decanters

These decanters show another type of cutting popular in Ireland after the turn of the nineteenth century. Pillar flutes in various designs were used extensively by Samuel Miller at the Waterford Glasshouse, but are sometimes to be seen on double handed cream bowls (piggins). These patterns are illustrated by Phelps Warren in his book *Irish Glass*, Plate 95 *et seq*. Other variations were alternate pillar and diamond cut pillar flutes and also the latter pattern alone. This type of cutting has a particularly brilliant effect, unlike any other, and the items are always of the finest quality. The shape of this decanter may well have developed from that of the modified cruciform decanter, with the panels now being of equal width and more deeply indented. Decanters would have been made in large matching sets, but it is now unusual to find more than pairs which have survived. Occasionally, it is interesting to note, engraved numbers appear on decanter and stopper, as each stopper was made to fit its decanter perfectly. The necks of the decanters illustrated are step cut and the stoppers are of the flat mushroom type with cut shaft and deep flutes. Height: 8″; date: *c.* 1810.

47

28 Flat Cut Early-Irish Decanter

An early-Irish flat cut pint sized decanter with deep mushroom stopper. Height: $9\frac{1}{2}''$; date: c. 1780.

This example shows typical kinds of flat cutting in vogue during the important Anglo-Irish period, 1770–1810. Cutting of this nature was widely used on all table glass in England and Ireland following its early invention about 1740.

The centre is cut with geometric patterns of which there were many variations. Above this band are four rows of unusual shaped facets, and at the base a band of narrow deep flutes. The rings on the neck also varied extensively and these greatly facilitated holding the decanter and filling glasses. In this case there are two, each made up of close triple collars. The stopper is decorated on the side with oval cut flutes and a 'wheel' of close flutes on top.

Cecil Davis Ltd

29 Quart Size Irish Decanter

This Irish decanter is decorated at the base with vertical moulded flutes, has a triple three-ringed neck and moulded mushroom stopper. Marked around the base in moulded letters is the inscription 'Waterloo Co. Cork'. Height: *c.* 8"; date: *c.* 1810. The fame of the Irish glass factories was kept alive for well over a century, and a great deal of glass has been erroneously attributed to Waterford, especially flat cut table ware with a greyish blue tinge. The principal Irish factories between 1760 and 1830 were located in Belfast, Cork, Dublin, and Waterford, and all marked some of their wares in capital letters in relief moulding. This is mainly seen on decanters, jugs and finger bowls. The most important manufacturer in Belfast was Benjamin Edwards who moved from Bristol to Drumea, Co. Tyrone, in 1771 and then to Belfast a few years later. He imported and employed English workmen who had been taught glassmaking at Bristol. His son Benjamin succeeded him, but the business suffered from the duties imposed on glass, even though in Ireland this was much lower than the tax in England. In Cork, some local men joined English employees in the opening of a glasshouse in 1783 which became the Cork Glass Co. The Waterloo Company was established in 1815 by Daniel Foley, and was run by him until he retired in

Richard Dennis

1830, whereafter the firm went bankrupt. In Dublin, a factory was opened in about 1674 by a Welsh family called Williams, and this lasted until 1827. Also working in the glass business here were Charles Mulvany, and John Dedereck Ayckbown who was from London. One of the first mentions of the Waterford Glass House was in a newspaper of 1783, in which it described the establishment as supplying all kinds of flint and plain glass, useful and ornamental.

30 Irish Straight Sided Decanter

An Irish quart sized decanter of straight-sided shape, decorated with a central band of diamond cutting, broad flutes on the shoulder, narrow flutes below, double cut slice cut neck, diamond cut mushroom stopper. Height: 10½"; date: c. 1810. This style decanter was made less frequently than the round type and is usually of heavier metal. After 1810 the vogue for more cutting on glass became marked, and a decade followed when diamond cutting and broad and narrow flute cutting on decanters and drinking glasses became very popular. On the former, bull's eye stoppers were most commonly used. The earlier sharp diamond cutting gave way after 1810 to a softer variation known as strawberry and rosette diamond cutting.

Cecil Davis Ltd

31 Irish Engraved Decanter

This pint size decanter is engraved on the body with typical simple festoon and star design of Neo-Classic inspiration. Vertical moulded flutes appear at the base, and it has a triple plain three-ringed neck, moulded bull's eye stopper and is marked 'Cork Glass Co.'. Height: *c.* 8″; date: *c.* 1810. It is interesting to note the great variety of types of rings on the necks of marked Irish decanters. The main types of rings applied are: triple plain curved rings; triple plain straight rings; triple faceted (cut) rings; triple three-ringed groups, triple milled (dented) moulded rings as in this illustration; and various moulded rings. The number of rings also varied. Usually three were applied, but also single, double, and occasionally quadruple groups are found. Another group was cut into the neck instead of being applied by a separate process.

Cannon Hall Art Gallery, Barnsley

32 Bristol Blue Decanter

A Bristol blue quart size decanter, decorated with narrow flutes at the base; double faceted ringed neck, and bull's eye stopper. Height: *c.* 10″; date: *c.* 1810. Although most blue glass of the English glassmaking period with which we are concerned is attributed to the Redcliffe Backs, Temple Meads, Bedminster and other factories in Bristol, it must be borne in mind that the production of blue glass took place in Ireland, and other parts of England. This decanter is unusual as the majority, although of the same pleasing simple shape, were decorated with gilt labels, (see Plate 23) and fitted with pear-shaped stoppers, while this example is without any gilding.

Richard Dennis

33 Irish Moulded Decanter

An Irish decanter with moulded mark around the base: 'Waterloo Co. Cork'. It is engraved with a conventional design of simple clear later Neo-Classic taste, has moulded flutes at the base, and a triple milled ringed neck. The stopper is flat and moulded. Moulded pieces of Irish origin for which the marks have been recorded are as follows:

B. Edwards. Belfast.
Cork Glass Co.
Waterloo Co. Cork.
J. D. Ayckbown. Dublin.
C.M.C.O. (Charles Mulvany, Dublin).
Penrose. Waterford.

Names on genuine pieces are quite often difficult to decipher and are sometimes missed. It would be well to be cautious of those glasses which seem heavier and bear large and easily legible letters, and to treat them with some suspicion. Height: 10″; date: *c.* 1810.

Richard Dennis

Derek C. Davis

34 Ship's Decanter

Obviously furniture and other items for use on board ship had to be especially adapted and suitably made. The requirements of the Navy and passenger lines did not escape the attention of the glassmaker, who consequently produced heavy decanters, claret and water jugs with wide bases. Glasses were usually fitted into wooden racks.

Some of these pieces were decorated with various types of cutting, as in this illustration, where the decanter (sometimes termed 'Rodney' decanter) is decorated on the shoulder with broad flutes and at the base with narrow ones; it has three plain rings on the neck and a mushroom stopper with a flattened ball shaft. Height: 8½"; date: *c.* 1810. Some ship's decanters were engraved, while others were left quite plain with triple ringed necks and bull's eye or pear-shaped stoppers. Semi-ship's decanters can also be found, but these are generally of a less elegant and heavier design, being more of a cone shape and usually flute cut from neck to base. Obviously, in spite of the adapted design for use on board ship, a large number of these pieces did not survive, and they are now difficult to find.

35 Georgian Carafe

A fine Georgian carafe, it bears a wheel engraved panel depicting Britannia with a ship to dexter and a lion sinister, flanked by emblems of war and ensigns. It has initials on the reverse, a base cut with narrow flutes, and a quadruple ringed slice cut neck. Height: 9″; date: *c.* 1810. Carafes or 'table water bottles' were, of course, principally used for wine, especially in the eighteenth and early-nineteenth centuries. As a carafe was first filled from the cellar and then immediately used at table, there was no need for a stopper, and the beauty of the glass can here be appreciated without the frosted section in the neck, which was produced by grinding the neck and stopper to ensure that a vessel would be airtight. Carafes were made in many different sizes, from the plain individual measure to magnum or even larger, and they were usually decorated with brilliant cutting. This carafe is a fine example of the recording of a patriotic picture on glass. The decorating of glass by engraving only really began to have a widespread popularity in England after about 1750 and the first picture motifs were labels naming the contents (see Plate 17). In the late-eighteenth and early-nineteenth centuries commemorative decoration proliferated; not only were domestic scenes recorded, such as the opening of the Iron Bridge over the River Wear, but gifts of plain goblets and decanters were engraved with the donor's or recipient's name or initials. There were also many engraved decanters recording the raising of volunteers for battles, visits to Yarmouth or such resorts, and toasting popular heroes such as Nelson the 'Brave Hero of the Nile'.

Richard Dennis

C. R. Butterworth

36 Georgian Spirit Decanter

This is one of a pair of Georgian pint size spirit decanters with bull's eye stoppers. It is of unusual squat shape, decorated with broad flute cutting and engraved crests. It is double lipped with triple rounded flute bands. Height: 7″; date: c. 1810.

The engraved crest on this decanter (and on its pair) is a feature of additional interest, as is the double lip. This type of lip may have been added by the glassmaker for the convenience of the user, but, like the single lipped decanters, it is not commonly found.

Derek C. Davis

37 Group of Miniature Decanters

This group again illustrates the diversity of the glass cutters' art, used to full advantage even on miniature decanters.

Left to right:

Rounded decanter waisted at the base, decorated with an intricate pattern of panel diamond cutting and flutes, single ringed neck and mushroom stopper, fluted base; *c.* 1820.

Miniature Irish ship's decanter decorated with bands of diamond and step cutting, mushroom stopper; *c.* 1820.

Plain decanter, triple ringed neck, bull's eye stopper; *c.* 1790.

Decanter decorated with broad and narrow flute cutting, double plain ringed neck, flat stopper; *c.* 1810.

Tapering Georgian decanter decorated with broad and narrow flute cutting, pear-shaped stopper; *c.* 1810.

Heights: $4\frac{1}{2}''-7\frac{1}{2}''$.

38 Irish Decanter

This straight-sided decanter is decorated with a cut design typical of the early-nineteenth-century Waterford factory. Height: 9½″; date: *c.* 1810. There are several types of flat cutting incorporated in this pattern, namely: close diamonds forming the arched panels with leaf and star motifs, broad flutes on the shoulder and narrow flutes at the base. The neck has three triple rings, and the decanter is fitted with a mushroom stopper. Sometimes this type of decanter is marked with the name of the factory (see Plates 31 and 33). Although unmarked, this example is probably from the Penrose Waterford company. The earliest reference to a glass house connected with Waterford was in the year 1729: the *Dublin Journal* of May 24th 1729 noted that 'The Glasshouse near Waterford (County Kilkenny) is now at work . . .'. In 1731, the owner John Head advertised the glass house emphasizing the supply of 'bottles with or without marks, . . . at the warehouse in Waterford'. On his death the factory was disposed of by letting. George and William Penrose established the most famous factory in Waterford in 1783, and the firm was held by the Penrose family until 1799. A dispute with the foreman and partner was one of the reasons for the then deputy foreman Jonathan Gatchell purchasing the firm, and thereafter the Gatchell family continued until the factory closed in 1851 whereafter the manufacture of flint glass in Waterford ceased.

Cecil Davis Ltd

39 Irish Claret Decanter

This is a splendid example of a claret decanter decorated with brilliant vertical
and horizontal step cutting. The lip is
also step cut, the handle slice cut, and
the rim serrated. The stopper is of the
diamond cut ball-shaped type, with flute
cutting on the top, which is echoed on
the base of the decanter. Height: 9″;
date: *c.* 1815. The late André Simon, a
well-known authority on wine, wrote
on the subject of claret; 'how is it that
claret, real claret, the red wine of Bordeaux, has been and still is, such a
favourite in every part of the civilized
world?

'For it is a very long time ago since the
bulk of the Bordeaux vintages were
shipped to England; they have, for
many years past and still have, a considerable number of admirers not only
in France, but also in the United States,
in Scandinavia and practically in every
corner of the world reached by civiliza-
tion. No other wine has had such a uni-
versal appeal for so long as claret. What
is the reason for it? Probably because
claret approaches nearer to perfect har-
mony than any other wine'. (*A Wine
Primer*, André Simon.)

Claret has been mentioned in history
many times and especially in lyrics referring to its fine qualities. It became
harder to find in the eighteenth century
when the Methuen Treaty encouraged

C. R. Butterworth

large quantities of Portuguese wines into England at the expense of French wines. It
is interesting to note that this form is something of a throwback to the early pottery
wine bottles of the seventeenth century, which had handles, as had the few early
bottle-decanters which were contemporaries of the Lambeth pottery jugs. Georgian
decanters with handles and pouring lips seem exclusively to be associated with
claret and are thus popularly called 'claret-jugs'.

Richard Dennis

40 Three George III Decanters

This set of three George III decanters (one quart and two pint size) illustrates an unusual combination of cutting and engraving. The decanters are of hunting interest, the oval panels being engraved, by the wheel method, with a fox and the inscription 'Tallio' and, on the reverse, with the initials 'G.J.A.'. The cutting is in the deep panel and strawberry diamond designs, the necks being step cut. The original flat mushroom stoppers are cut with panels and with slice cut shafts. Height: 8″–10″; date: *c.* 1815.

Many events were recorded on glass, such as the institution of clubs and societies, as it was natural that decanters and glasses, to be used at dinners and other functions, should be chosen for this purpose.

41 Octagonal Irish Decanter

This decanter is a good example of one decorated with step cutting. The technique produced a particularly brilliant effect as each ridge reflects the next. This type of cutting was characteristic of 1815 and proved very popular because of its silvery effect. This decanter is probably from the Waterford factory but it is not possible to be certain. Height: 6½″; date: 1815.

The type of cutting shown here was used with splendid results on all sorts of table glass, especially upon dishes of varying shapes. The effect was further enhanced at night by candlelight and when used with silver tableware which increased the reflection of light.

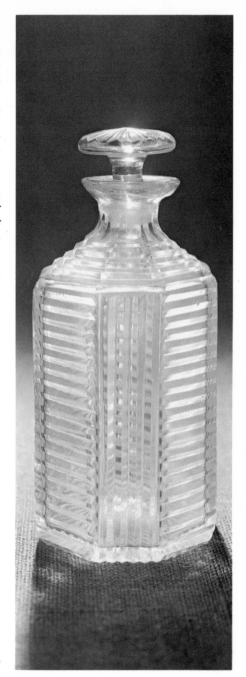

Cecil Davis Ltd

Cannon Hall Art Gallery, Barnsley

42 Panel Cut Georgian Decanter

This is a typical specimen although made less frequently than those with ringed necks. The outline is perhaps more effective, slightly barrel-shaped and sloping up to the lip in graduated cut flute collars instead of applied rings, the style which was more often advertised by the glass traders. The vertical panel cutting which decorates the body of the decanter was formed by pillar flutes and close diamond cutting which required precision of the highest degree. The base is flute cut, and the mushroom type of stopper which was so fashionable in the latter years of George III's reign has a slice cut shaft. Height: 9″; date: *c*. 1820; capacity one pint.

43 Straight Sided Decanter

This quart size Georgian decanter illustrates decoration using only one type of cutting, consisting of broad flutes extending over the entire surface of the decanter, and which is described by the term 'slice cut'. The octagonal stopper is also slice cut. Height: 10″; date: *c.* 1820. The stems of early-nineteenth-century wine glasses were often decorated in this way. Slice cutting was more infrequently executed on bottles and decanters as patterns of diamonds, but the range of design was extremely varied, according to the ideas of the craftsmen and the popularity assessed from the number of sales.

Cecil Davis Ltd

44 Regency Bottle Shaped Decanter

The brilliant decoration on this quart size decanter consists of diamond cutting with steps above and below. The neck has a single ring and the ball-shaped stopper is cut with deep flutes, with a similar decoration on the base. This is a particularly graceful example of the bottle-shaped decanter. Before cutting, the vessel would be made in plain glass of almost double the thickness required, and the vessel if not cut at the glass house itself was probably cut in the vicinity. These decanters would probably have been made in sets of twelve or more. Height: $11\frac{1}{2}''$; date *c.* 1820.

45 Square Irish Decanter

Comparatively few decanters of square design were made in the eighteenth and early-nineteenth centuries either in England or Ireland. There is a pair of very rare magnum Irish decanters of this shape in the Alexander Collection, Walton-on-the-Hill, the only pair recorded of this size and shape.

There seems to be no apparent reason for the lack of decanters of this shape apart from the fact that it was a great era for drinking port, whereas this shape would be more suitable for spirits. After 1830 the square design became far more popular and, in Victorian times, pairs or sets of three were fitted into a wooden frame with metal handles above, with a section on a hinge at the base and complete with a lock and key. Such a set, known as a tantalus, kept the bottles and contents safe from the inquisitive! (See Plate 53.)

The decanter in this illustration is decorated with four kinds of cutting in frequent use just after 1800. The shoulder is cut with flutes, the wide band with strawberry diamonds and, below that, bands of circular flutes and alternate slanting close diamonds and flutes. Height: $7\frac{1}{2}''$; date: c. 1820. The mushroom stopper is original and is decorated with strawberry diamond and flute cutting.

Other pairs of square quart size decanters decorated with similar cutting have also been recorded, and heavy plain square decanters with faceted ball shaped stoppers were made from about 1840 onwards.

Derek C. Davis

C. R. Butterworth

46 Georgian Decanter of Pedestal Shape

This attractive design was sometimes used as an alternative to the more common shapes of the first quarter of the nineteenth century, which were not waisted at the base. The central band of diamonds on this decanter has been expertly cut over the rounded surface with broad flutes above and below. The neck has double plain rings and the stopper is of the usual mushroom type. Rounded diamond cut stoppers would originally have been fitted. These decanters were always of the finest quality and can be found fairly regularly in both full and half bottle sizes. The subtle change of form seen in this example is a foretaste of the later-nineteenth century exaggeration of earlier shapes. Height: $7\frac{1}{2}''$; date: *c.* 1820.

47 Victorian Claret Decanter

This claret jug, decorated with heavy panel cutting, straight sided and with a flat cartwheel stopper, is representative of some of the Victorian ungainliness of proportion. The clumsiness seems the more striking after the elegance and beauty of the Georgian glasses. This change in style became more and more apparent and culminated in the 1851 Great Exhibition, where over-embellishment and garish decorations on glass were abundantly exhibited by many manufacturers. This fashion persisted throughout the century until some of the more austere products of the Art Nouveau movement in the early-twentieth century brought about a change. The cartwheel stopper though not common at any time had been used earlier, but was most popular in the 1840s. Height: 11½″; date: c. 1840.

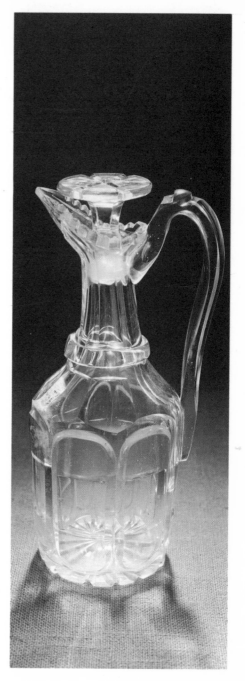

Cecil Davis Ltd

48 Early-Victorian Decanter

This quart size decanter is one of a pair, with a handled claret jug *en suite*. Matching sets are not often found, but different styles often go well together and glasses and decanters can be bought in sufficient numbers to form a suite of table glass. The decanter illustrated is decorated with deep vertical flutes, the neck is slice cut with a large flattened collar at the base and just above the shoulder. This stopper is a variation of the earlier familiar mushroom style, being cut with wide flutes and octagonal in shape. As usual at this period, glasses and decanters were made of thick metal and were consequently heavy when used. Even on this restrained example one can see changes in relative proportions, tending towards the exaggeration associated with the Victorian era, which may account for the decanters of the mid-nineteenth century not being as much favoured as earlier productions. Height: *c.* 10″; date: *c.* 1840.

Cecil Davis Ltd

49 Victorian Apple Green Decanter

This unusual colour apple green decanter is of octagonal shape, and decorated with broad flutes and step cutting, and rounded flute cut stopper. The neck has a single plain ring and the base is decorated with close flat cutting. Height: 7″; date: *c.* 1840. A marked characteristic of the early-Victorian period up to 1850 was the brightly coloured table glass, which, although now not always considered to be in very good taste, had a remarkable variety in design. Stourbridge has always been noted for a large output of glass, and, as early as the mid-eighteenth century a traveller in the Midlands noted: 'we came to Stourbridge, famous for its glass manufacture, especially for its coloured glass'. A pattern book still exists, in the museum of the firm Stevens and Williams at Brierley Hill, which contains a long list of coloured glass being used for layered or cased glassware and as an alternative to cut glass patterns.

During the nineteenth century in Central Europe, there was a great vogue for coloured glass, particularly stained glass, a technique known by the term 'Biedermeier' by which stains were fired on to the surface of the glass. This staining produced a less dense effect, as in the decanter illustrated, and was particularly effective if landscapes and designs

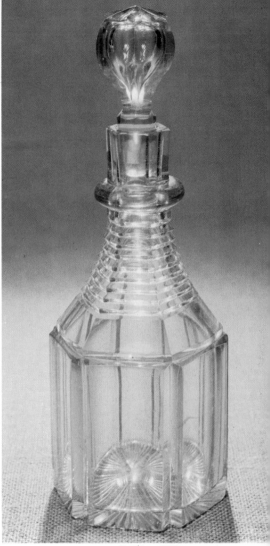

Cecil Davis Ltd

were added. The English manufacturers at first showed some reluctance to use coloured glasses (perhaps because they were justly proud of their fine lead glass), but towards 1850 the popularity of coloured glass encouraged the manufacture. It was not long before it was very fashionable, with an enormous output from firms such as Richardsons of Stourbridge, Bacchus and Son, and Lloyd and Summerfield of Birmingham.

69

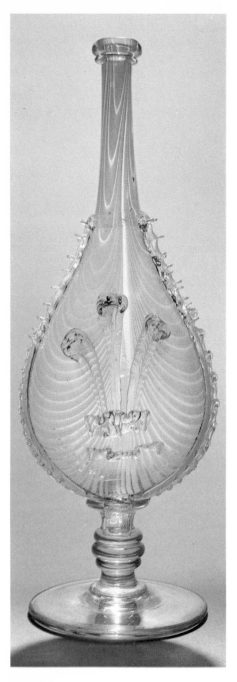

50 Ornamental Bellows Flask

In the early part of the nineteenth century, quantities of common coloured glass were made for various uses, including the manufacture of novelties. Of the latter type, a considerable amount has come to be called Nailsea Ware, as the name of this small town near Bristol has long been associated with items of crude bottle glass and of other glasses of better metal. A great deal of the Nailsea Wares were of bottle glass 'of rural style' with the most common decoration being of white or coloured glass splashes, applied to jugs, decanters, bottles, and mugs, which were intended for practical table use. Another decorative motif, derived ultimately from Venetian Lattimo glass, was formed by white or coloured bands of opaque glass being applied to the newly blown glass bubble before complete inflation. These bands became integrated with the surface of the vessel and were tooled into waves or festoons for decorative effect. The glass was sometimes also decorated with applied pincered decoration or spiral trailing. The piece illustrated here is a particularly fine example in the form of a bellows, and is decorated with white opaque festoons, and trailed pincered work on the sides, with a Prince of Wales' feather motif in the centre. Much of the glass, particularly the early material, was made elsewhere, notably in Shropshire, and it is possible that this example could have been made at the Bank Quay Glassworks in Warrington. There is a similar specimen in the Municipal Museum and Art Gallery in Warrington. Height: 15"; date: c. 1840.

Worthing Museum and Art Gallery

51 Heavy Green Decanter

A clear glass decanter of heavy metal, flashed with green, it is mallet shaped and deeply cut with steps, V-shaped flute panels, oval flutes and broad flutes at the base: it has a cut pinnacle stopper containing a large air 'tear'. The 'flashed' technique of colouring glass was the fusing of a thin coating of coloured glass on to plain glass. Height: $12\frac{1}{4}''$; date: *c.* 1850.

This decanter also shows the ungainly development in Victorian design and, as it is made of heavy metal it would not be very practical for use, especially when filled! It is interesting to note the shape of this particular decanter; the heavy mallet shape in the Victorian era was of short duration, and was soon replaced by the well-known and equally ungainly globular type.

Cecil Davis Ltd

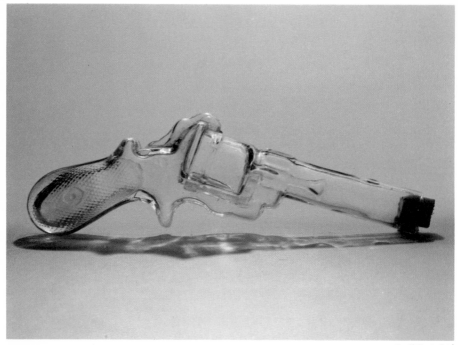

52 Moulded 'Pistol' Flask

Many glass novelties were made in the nineteenth century, both in coloured and clear metal. Some were purely decorative, illustrating the glassmaker's art, and took the form of hats, walking sticks, bugles, tobacco pipes, rolling pins, shoes, etc., and were known colloquially as 'friggers'. Other items were given a practical purpose, such as this hollow flask in the form of a pistol, which may possibly have been sold as a souvenir at an exhibition or fair to advertise some brand of soft drink or spirit. The attention to detail is good, for example corks were used instead of glass stoppers, and they were easy to carry around and convenient to use when required. Date: *c.* 1860. There is a very good collection of these friggers in the Stourbridge collection. Nailsea glass was frequently used in the manufacture of these amusing novelties (see Plate 50), some of which have become associated with superstitions. It was believed, for example, that if glass walking sticks were hung near a window and washed or cleaned regularly, the house would be free from bad luck and particularly protected from fevers or similar illnesses. The glass would attract the evil influence which could then be washed away.

Derek C. Davis

53 Rare Miniature Tantalus

A good example of a travellers' sample, or alternatively a set for liqueurs. Towards the end of the eighteenth century, square based, straight sided decanters were being made, sometimes in sets in metal frames similar to those used for sauce and condiment bottles. (See Plate 45.) Most often they were made in coloured glass with cut and gilt decoration, and it is generally believed that they originated from Bristol. The fashion reached its greatest popularity in Victorian times, when sets of three or four vessels in heavily cut clear glass were placed in an open wood container, the lower part of which could be locked so that the bottles could not be moved without a key, as in the illustration. It is possible that they were made at Stourbridge, but there are no marks on wood, metal or glass confirming this. Height: bottles, 5", frame, $7\frac{1}{4}$"; date: c. 1860. This type of object illustrates the ingenuity and general complexity of design so typical of the Victorian era, in all types of furnishing and art, which did so much to aid the overcrowded appearance of the average Victorian living room.

54 Dome Shaped Decanter

This late-Victorian quart size decanter of an unusual domed shape illustrates the drastic change in design and appearance since the beginning of the nineteenth century. It is engraved with alternate floral and leaf motifs above which is a band of 'tongue' engraving. The latter is a late recurrence of a popular late-eighteenth-century style. The neck is decorated with another pattern used over two centuries, that of the growing vine, produced by wheel engraving. Height: $11\frac{1}{2}''$; date: $c.$ 1880.

The curious circular hollow stopper is both notch cut and etched, a term which covers a wide range of different kinds of treatment to which the surface of the glass is subjected. In this case parts of the glass are protected by wax, resin or a similar substance, whilst the glass is dipped into a solution of hydrofluoric acid for ten minutes. Where the glass is unprotected the etched effect appears.

Cecil Davis Ltd

74

55 Green Glass Scent Bottle

This charming little scent bottle, which
is probably from Bristol, exemplifies the
quiet dignity and quality of the products
of the eighteenth century, and the very
best of the skill of English craftsmen.
The surface is covered in facets and
decorated with a criss-cross gilt design.
The spirally fluted silver cap covers a
tiny glass stopper. This particular example is still complete with its original
case made of shark skin, and as a fortu-
nate result the gilt design, so accurately
applied, is in fine condition. So many
designs on other types of coloured glass,
especially decanters, have been partly
rubbed away in spite of the fact that the
gilt was fired on. Height: 3″; width: 1½″;
date: *c.* 1770. The mid-eighteenth century manufacture in Bristol of glass
scent bottles was closely related to experiments there in porcelain making. In
1750 a factory making porcelain from
soapstone was established in Bristol. At
the same time opaque-white glass vessels,
including enamelled scent bottles were
produced, and these continued to be
made there until the end of the century.
Facet cut bottles such as our example
were also made there, and have often
been called after the town. The colours
found in these bottles are blue and green
with amethyst being the rarest. Faceted
examples were sometimes also enamelled
with bright chinoiserie scenes or with
birds and figures. Occasionally exquisite
miniature sets of four, fitted in open-
work gilt metal cases, usually about 2″
high, were also made.

Cecil Davis Ltd

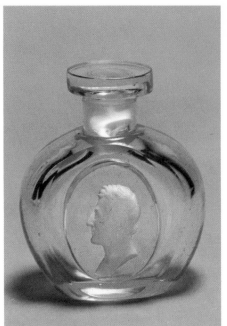

56 Apsley Pellatt Bottle

Most items inset with Apsley Pellatt cameo subjects were decorated with brilliant diamond cutting. The bottle shown is unusual, being of plain glass. Height: $3\frac{1}{2}''$; date: *c.* 1820.

Cameo encrustation entailed the extremely skilled operation of maintaining exactly the right temperatures for the cameo and for the glass pocket into which it is introduced. Whilst the end of the glass on the rod is rewarmed, the workman exhausts the air, the glass and cameo becoming welded together.

Apsley Pellatt, owner of a glass house in Southwark, patented in 1819 his method of producing silvery looking profile portraits. Known as sulphides, they were made of a special porcelain that would not crack when brought into contact with molten glass.

57 Blue Opaline Scent Bottle

It will be noticed that the gilt design on this bottle shows only slight wear as it is of the fired technique. This means that the object is first made and then gilded, being finally fired again at a slightly lower temperature to make the gilding as permanent as possible. Height: $4\frac{1}{2}''$; date: *c.* 1860.

The earlier technique was known as 'cold' painting or gilding, by which the object was not fired again after the design had been applied and a large number of important crests, coats-of-arms and inscriptions have consequently worn away. Other opaline colours used fairly frequently during this period were light green, royal blue, and ruby.

Richard Dennis (above): Cecil Davis Ltd (below)

Derek C. Davis

58 Early-nineteenth-century Scent Bottles

Diamond cutting, so popular at that time, is shown in various forms on these examples. It is especially well executed on the clear glass example in the centre on which the decoration is graduated from the base to neck. The same example has a gilt screw top engraved with a family crest, and there is a tiny glass stopper inside. Both the other examples are in colours of glass uncommonly found in the Georgian period, the rarer being the pink bottle, which has an almost twentieth-century shape. Both have original stoppers. The most unusual colours found in Georgian glass of this period 1820–30, are pinks or deeper ruby shades with amber colours being slightly more common. All three examples were probably made at Stourbridge. Height: centre bottle, $3\frac{1}{2}''$; date: c. 1830. Coloured glass which had been popular for some time in Bohemia only began to achieve some popularity in England just before the Great Exhibition of 1851. At the exhibition, the range of colours advertised by the manufacturers was as follows; jewel-stone colours, brown, black, yellow, green, blue, pink, red, ruby, and purple. By the later part of the nineteenth century, the output, especially from centres such as Stourbridge, was enormous, and the range and combinations of colours very wide.

59 Stourbridge Cameo Scent Bottles

Mrs Susanna Tillman

These small scent bottles illustrate the extremely expert carving in white glass on three of the main colour grounds used (the fourth being turquoise). Height: $3\frac{1}{4}$–4″; date: c. 1880. The technique involved in making these vessels was long and complicated; first a translucent coloured background was blown and then covered with an opaque layer of white glass, which was then painstakingly cut away to leave the usually floral cameo pattern. The slow process of cameo carving, derived from the Romans, was speeded up in the nineteenth century by the use of acid and mechanical carving tools although the final carving had to be carefully controlled by hand. Items in this technique were frequently commissioned by collectors or for exhibitions and could take years from start to finish, costing a great deal, but perhaps the best known are the small decorative items. Webb and Richardson were the two firms at Stourbridge which were concerned with this work, the most famous craftsmen being John Northwood and George and Thomas Woodall. The style attracted American interest, and a few Stourbridge artists emigrated to do similar work there. The Mt. Washington Glass Company in Massachusetts produced cameo glass, but there was not a great deal of concern over carving and shading. At the end of the nineteenth century the technique was developed to sumptuous effect by French glassmakers, especially Emile Gallé, and occasionally the technique was practised by the master glassmakers of Louis Comfort Tiffany in New York.

60 Intaglio Scent Bottle

Richard Dennis

This charming Georgian scent bottle, *c.* 1820, bears an intaglio portrait of Queen Adelaide and is an extremely interesting variation of the work of Apsley Pellatt, being intaglio cut rather than cameo encrustation. James Tassie, the remarkable gem engraver from Scotland, began experimenting with methods of reproducing his cameo portraits. He was already well known for his cutting of glass gems but with the help of his nephew William Tassie, he began to produce miniature portraits in white glass paste in the early-nineteenth century. Apsley Pellatt, the most famous maker of glass paste cameos and sulphides, wrote a book in 1821 which was revised in 1849, *The Memoirs on the origin and improvement of glass manufactures including the patent crystallo ceramie or glass encrustation.* He mentions that the first man to experiment in that field was a Bohemian manufacturer who attempted to encrust in glass small figures of greyish clay with apparently no great success. In the early-nineteenth century a Frenchman, Desprez, began producing high quality portraits in a porcellanous material and by the early years of the century had succeeded in encasing them in glass (see Plate 56). These reliefs took on a rather silvery appearance once embedded in glass, and although at first they were used as framed objects to be hung, they subsequently came to be attached into the sides of beakers, cream jugs, scent bottles, and decanters. Apsley Pellatt, as we have noted, was most interested in the technique and patented his method of encasing sulphides in 1819. A man named Charles Brown seems to have been associated in making cameos with both Pellatt and Tassie, particularly in the making of some of the glass cameo profiles, and it may be possible that he had a hand in engraving this portrait of Queen Adelaide wife of William IV. This example is one of a wide range of bottles bearing portraits of notable people. The Pellatt glasses were almost always marked Pellatt and Co. Patentees, and the portraits almost always surrounded, as on this example, with a decorative border of the classical honeysuckle pattern. The bottle is finely cut with diamonds and deep flutes and has its original stopper. Apsley Pellatt showed examples of some of his own glass cameos in the 1851 exhibition, but they do not seem to have met with much enthusiasm, the technique not being quite so novel by that time.

SELECT BIBLIOGRAPHY

ASH, Douglas, *How to Identify English Drinking Glasses and Decanters*, Bell, London, 1962; Clarke Irwin, New York
CROMPTON, Sydney, *English Glass*, Ward Lock, 1967
ELVILLE, E. M., *English Table Glasses*, Country Life, London, 1951; *English and Irish Cut Glass*, Country Life, London, 1954: *Collectors' Dictionary of Glass*, Country Life; Tudor, New York, 1970
HAYNES, E. Barrington, *Glass Through The Ages*, Pelican, London, 1948
HONEY, W. B., *English Glass*, Victoria and Albert Museum, 1946
HUGHES, G. Bernard, *English, Scottish and Irish Table Glass*, Batsford, London, 1956
LLOYD, Ward, *Investing in Georgian Glass*, The Cresset Press, London, 1969; Clarkson N. Potter, New York
RUGGLES-BRISE, Sheelah, *Sealed Bottles*, Country Life, London; Scribners', New York, 1949
THORPE, W. A., *A History of English and Irish Glass* (2 Vols.), Medici Society, London, 1929; Saifer, New York, 1970: *English Glass*, A. & C. Black, London, 1935; B. & N., New York, 1961; *English and Irish Glass*, Medici Society, London, 1927
WARREN, Phelps, *Irish Glass*, Faber and Faber, 1970
WESTROPP, M. S. D., *Irish Glass*, Herbert Jenkins, London, 1920
WILLS, Geoffrey, *Pocket Book of Glass*, Country Life, 1966; Hawthorn, New York, 1966: *English and Irish Glass* (Vols. 1–16), Guinness, London, 1968; Doubleday, New York, 1970

COLLECTIONS ON VIEW

Europe
AUSTRIA. Vienna: Kunsthistorisches Museum, Museum für Angewandte Kunst
BELGIUM. Brussels: Musées Royaux d'Art et d'Histoire; Liege: Musée d'Archéologie et d'Arts
CZECHOSLOVAKIA. Liberec: Severočeské Museum; Prague: Uměleckoprumislové Museum
DENMARK. Copenhagen: C. L. Davids Museum, Det Danske Kunstindustre Museum
GERMANY. Berlin, East and West: Kunstgewerbe Museums; Cologne: Kunstgewerbe Museum; Dusseldorf: Kunstmuseum; Frankfurt: Museum für Kunsthandwerk; Hamburg: Museum für Kunst und Gewerbe; Munich: Bayerisches Staatsgemälde Sammlung; Nuremburg: Germanisches Nat. Museum
FRANCE. Nancy: Musée des Beaux-Arts; Paris: Louvre, Musée des Arts Décoratifs
HOLLAND. Amsterdam: Rijksmuseum; Hague: Haags Gemeentemuseum; Rotterdam: Museum Buymans-van Beuningen
HUNGARY. Budapest: Iparmivezeti Muzeum
NORWAY. Oslo: Kunstrimuseet i Oslo
REPUBLIC OF IRELAND. Dublin: National Museum
SWEDEN. Stockholm: Staters Historika Museum
SWITZERLAND. Basle: Gewerbemuseum; Geneva: Musée d'Art et d'Histoire; Zurich: Kunstgewerb Museum
UNITED KINGDOM. Bedford: Cecil Higgins Museum; Belfast: Ulster Museum; Bristol: City Museum and Art Gallery; Cambridge: Fitzwilliam Museum; Cardiff: National Museum of Wales; Edinburgh: Royal Scottish Museum; Exeter: Royal Albert Memorial Museum; London: British Museum, Guildhall Museum, London Museum, Victoria and Albert Museum; Norwich: Strangers Hall, Castle Museum; Manchester: City Art Gallery; Oxford: Ashmolean Museum; Saint Helens: Pilkington Glass Museum; Stourbridge: Stourbridge Borough Collection

North America
CANADA. Toronto: Royal Ontario Museum
U.S.A Baltimore, Md.: Baltimore Museum of Art; Boston, Mass.: Museum of Fine Art; Chicago, Ill.: Art Institute of Chicago; Cleveland, Ohio: Cleveland Museum of Art; Minneapolis, Minn.: Institute of Arts; Corning, N.Y.: Corning Museum of Glass; New York: Brooklyn Museum, Metropolitan Museum of Art; Jamestown, Va.: Museum of Jamestown; Philadelphia, Pa.: Museum of Art; Richmond, Va.: Association for the Preservation of Virginia; Toledo, Ohio: Museum of Art; Washington, D.C.: Smithsonian Institute; Williamsburg, Va.: Colonial Williamsburg